Send Them Victorious

Victorious

England's Path To Glory

2006 - 2010

T0050524

Send Them Victorious

Victorious

England's Path To Glory
2006 - 2010

David Stubbs

BOOKS

Winchester, UK
Washington, USA

First published by O-Books, 2010

O Books is an imprint of John Hunt Publishing Ltd., The Bothy, Deershot Lodge, Park Lane, Ropley, Hants, SO24 0BE, UK
office1@o-books.net
www.o-books.com

Distribution in:

UK and Europe
Orca Book Services Ltd
Home trade orders
tradeorders@orcabookservices.co.uk
Tel: 01235 465521
Fax: 01235 465555

Export orders
exportorders@orcabookservices.co.uk
Tel: 01235 465516 or 01235 465517
Fax: 01235 465555

USA and Canada
NBN
custserv@nbnbooks.com
Tel: 1 800 462 6420 Fax: 1 800 338 4550

Australia and New Zealand
Brumby Books
sales@brumbybooks.com.au
Tel: 61 3 9761 5535 Fax: 61 3 9761 7095

Far East (offices in Singapore, Thailand, Hong Kong, Taiwan)
Pansing Distribution Pte Ltd
kemal@pansing.com
Tel: 65 6319 9939 Fax: 65 6462 5761

South Africa
Stephan Phillips (pty) Ltd
Email: orders@stephanphillips.com
Tel: 27 21 4489839 Telefax: 27 21 4479879

Text copyright David Stubbs 2009

ISBN: 978 1 84694 457 4

Design: Stuart Davies

A CIP catalogue record for this book is available from the British Library.

Printed by Digital Book Print

O Books operates a distinctive and ethical publishing philosophy in all areas of its business, from its global network of authors to production and worldwide distribution.

Cover illustration by Ed Carter.
Thanks to Jack Seale and to the One Touch Football community
at When Saturday Comes for support and encouragement

INTRODUCTION

If it is true that football is "the continuation of war by other means", as George Orwell had it, then no one has taken that maxim more admirably to heart than the "Wing Commander". His full name cannot be revealed for security purposes – although he has not been on active service for some years, his distinguished career (which began with the Boer War) has seen him involved, like some pluckier Flashman, in all the major skirmishes of the last 100 or so years. He fought on both sides of the Spanish Civil War, doubtless alongside Mr Orwell, on a mission to kill as many Spaniards as possible regardless of political hue. He rode with the White Russians, was involved in a discreet cull of GIs during the beach invasion at Normandy and even discharged his weapon on German leftist terrorists in the early 70s, though military historians now agree that he most likely stumbled into a Kraftwerk concert by mistake under the influence of schnapps.

Since 2006, exacting assistance from his faithful and melancholy retainer Seppings, the Wing Commander has dedicated his retirement to writing up match reports on every England international, be it friendly, European qualifier or at the World Cup finals themselves. They follow England's progress from their World Cup 2006 campaign in which, among others, they overcame the mighty Trinidad & Tobago, to their mystifying absence from Euro 2008 and their scarcely impeded progress to the 2010 World Cup, despite the absurd handicap of having some bewildered Italian waiter, barely capable of speaking, as their manager. They have appeared on the website of the footballing magazine of note When Saturday Comes and have garnered a dedicated and appreciative audience. For these are no ordinary reports. They do not dwell morbidly and, some would argue, unpatriotically on any failings in England's performances. They are not mere blow-by-blow accounts of the game. There are no player ratings. Rather, they seek to show how highly England rates as a nation, in terms of breeding, deportment, erect carriage, pluck. They seek to instil these values into the young men of what remains of the Empire – to reawaken our sense of inherent superiority and entitlement, which is revived every few years across the country in the run-up to every international tournament for which England have qualified, when the St George's flags are laid out like bunting in every street, hamlet, village and town, when optimism and high expectation are at their most resurgent in every hale and hearty young lad about town. These values transcend football, indeed make the playing of the game an irrelevance; as the Wing Commander points out, it is difficult for referees to award a free kick to England rather than play advantage since, being English, they are always an advantage.

By contrast, the Wing Commander casts a withering eye on England's foreign opponents. They emerge very poorly from these reports – jabbering, swarthy, impertinent in their attempts to jostle England off the ball at every opportunity. The playing of the national anthems generally reveals to the Wing Commander their species inferiority. So magisterial is our own tune and its lusty rendering by John Terry, Rio Ferdinand et al that it blasts the random parps and mewlings that constitute foreign anthems to Kingdom Come. So comprehensively is England's superiority affirmed that it is a wonder, and indeed an affront, that the game is subsequently played at all – as if there were something further left to prove.

To read these match reports is not merely to be thrilled at England's ever-winning ways and revel in their unbroken sequence of triumphs on the field of play. They serve also as invaluable historical, international, sociological and racial biological guides, telling you, in effect, all you need to know about other countries, their customs, follies, peculiarities and odours. They assess and evaluate each nation's heritage, meagre as it may be. Take this extract from a report of a "friendly" against the age-old low country foe The Netherlands.

"Ah, England, my England. Literally my England, in the case of several thousand acres of it, as numerous backpacking trespassers have had cause to reflect upon as they pick buckshot out of the seat of their corduroys. What has England bequeathed to the world? The Bard of Avon. The four-minute mile. The sandwich. Gravity. Football, both codes. Penicillin. Electricity. Common sense. Field Marshall Montgomery. Fair play. Benevolent colonial rule. The Penny Farthing. The lavatory. Rudyard Kipling. High tea. The fagging system. The grimy chimney sweep. The finest navy on the high seas. Her Royal Highness the late Princess Margaret. The oratory of Winston Churchill. "Land of Hope and Glory". The steam engine. The industrial revolution. What, by contrast, have our foes upon the footballing field this night, the Dutch, given us? Elm disease."

From Ecuador to Estonia, from Israel to the former colony presently known as the United States of America, from Greece to Germany, each of our would-be foreign competitors is given similarly short shrift, skewered with similar acuity on the quill nib of the Wing Commander.

He scotches too the idea that the England team are in any way a spoiled, overrated, lax coalition of visually repugnant, clueless mediocrities with all the tactical nous of the Charge of the Light Brigade, whose disappointing performances in major tournaments are as inevitable as their inability to take on board any lessons from their failures, whose hyperbole, inflated wages and celebrity status far outweigh their actual talent or skill. No such talk in these reports. Others may find humour in Paul Robinson's goalkeeping howlers, Rio Ferdinand's lapses of concentration, Wayne Rooney's resemblance to an angry potato, Peter Crouch's resemblance to a swastika when attempting a scissors kick – not the Wing Commander, who only draws attention to such things in order to refute them. John Terry in particular excites his admiration: "Mr Bulldog" himself, the very embodiment of all that is English and manly, and who inspires some of the author's more crimson, ardent prose, effusive praise that seems to spring at times from the venerable old man's very loins.

It's not fanciful to say that these reports, taken as a whole, represent a veritable Bayeux tapestry of footballing achievement and continuing proof of the intrinsic superiority of England and the English, which makes a mockery of any anomalous statistic to the contrary on the scoreboard. But here, it is the foreigners who take one in the eye, time and again, as English spunk prevails.

Interspersed with these reports, however, are the wise words and reflections of a selection of other characters who are themselves a key part of the English footballing tapestry. There is, for example, HUGH McLAUGHTON, the broadsheet correspondent, who repeatedly deplores the pampered effeminacy of the modern game and yearns on a weekly basis for the days when footballing men were hewn from the granite of the auld Scotland, and wore voluminous shorts which doubled up as tents for their annual camping holidays. HARTLEY SEBAG-FFIENNES, the Arsenal supporter and florid North London aesthete who believes Arsenal should be renamed "Artenal", their games featured on The South Bank Show not Match Of The Day, a team for whom the pitch is their canvas and the Emirates their easel, whose artistry contrasts with the crude, base daubs of their regional opposition. INAPPROPRIATE CHAMPIONSHIP MANAGER, who in post-match interviews muses on every defeat with extended similes that reveal a somewhat lively, unorthodox, some might even say appallingly depraved private life. ("It's a bit like dog crucifixion.") SELF-RIGHTEOUS LIVERPOOL FAN, for whom every Liverpool setback is a cue to open a Book of Condolences, as well as solemn promises to rise again, as a city, with all the hearts, guts, passion and guts of a truly special city, home to such talents as Stan Boardman, Carla

Lane and Tom O'Connor. And finally, there is TOMMY SUNDERLAND, the unfortunately surnamed Newcastle United supporter, whose own personal bad luck mirrors that of his team as they suffer relegation to the First Division, but who remains optimistic that with Alan Shearer at the helm and Michael Owen leading the charge, they'll bounce straight back.

All these men of letters offer proof perfect to generations both present and future that the British game is in rude health. And even if it is not always healthy, there is at least rudeness in abundance.

David Stubbs

ENGLAND MATCH REPORTS

ENGLAND V JAMAICA - Friendly
June 3, 2006

Routine home victory for England in pre-World Cup warm-up. Peter Crouch celebrates a hat-trick with a silly dance.

MAGNIFICENT ENGLAND SHOW JAMAICA WHO ARE THE MASTERS ONCE MORE 6-0

In the 17th century, kindly English visitors landed at the shores of the jewel island of Jamaica and taught its inhabitants, both indigenous and imported, the value of sugar production, and how it might feed a mighty empire in providing a sweetener for such sacred ceremonies as the daily partaking of high tea. Today, as high tea was declared across England it was done so in the knowledge that members of a former colony had been delivered, for their own good, a sound thrashing, the welts of which will act as a reminder to this obstreperous people of their folly in presuming to determine their own destiny, independent of the guidance of Her Majesty The Queen's representatives.

In truth, this footballing contest was decided the moment the kits were laid out. England's bold, red colours were consciously reminiscent of the triumph of 1966 when, for a third time, we put our Teutonic cousins and foes in their place. Red is the colour of Empire. Jamaica, by contrast, played in yellow shirts. It is hard to think of any footballing nation that has won the World Cup sporting such naively garish colours.

As for the national anthems, the Jamaicans' was sung by a gentleman by the name of Jimmy Cliff. It is touching, perhaps, that Mr Cliff took his name from our own Cliff Richard, but also somewhat presumptuous of him to imagine that he was a singer of the same order. It was remarkably restrained of the English fans merely to boo his performance.

The Jamaican team are managed by a gentleman by the name of Wendell Downswell. Clearly, it took our players a few minutes to calm down from laughing at this, for in the meantime, the Jamaicans - forgetting, I fancy, that they were guests in this country - attempted a few attacks on the English goal for their insolence. Fortunately, sanity was restored as Frank Lampard thundered home a goal which put down this short-lived field rebellion.

Thereafter, the game was a reminder of happier, more sensible times, with the English occupying Jamaica in their own territory, David Beckham a veritable governor in a metaphorical plumed hat commanding affairs from the white pillared mansion of his innate superiority, with the Jamaicans themselves doing most of the work in building up England's wealth in the goal tally. Things as they were and as they should be.

England continued to dominate in the second half; so much so that key players such as Sol Campbell could afford to entertain the crowd with his amusing impersonation of a useless, paceless lummox who shouldn't be anywhere near the England squad, while Steven Gerrard sensibly converted the occasion into an exercise in energy conservation.

Perhaps the most touching gesture came from Peter Crouch. On being awarded a penalty, he forsook the chance of completing his hat trick. Rather, seeing the happy, shining face of a young England fan in the seats behind the goal, he deliberately lobbed the ball over the bar into his hands so that he might keep it as a souvenir of the game. The Jamaicans whooped, too unsophisticated to understand a gesture of magnanimity when they see one; this is the English way of doing things.

The Jamaican team were, naturally, contemptible and wretched. The only chance they would have had of reducing the goal tally would have been to lower the bar to "limbo dancing" level - and don't think these scoundrels wouldn't have tried to do so had it not been for the watchful, overseeing eye of the referee!

For the Jamaicans, smiling widely despite their poor lot, 6-0 will be a more than satisfactory result. No doubt in their own country, a national holiday will be declared to celebrate that they kept the score to under 10. (Though should they take a break from work, who will notice the difference? That remark was intended in amusement, a humorous diversion, though of course, it is essentially quite serious.)

Make no mistake. It is clear upon the basis of this superlative performance that England will indubitably win the World Cup, and that the official FIFA engraver should at once be set to work on the trophy, rather than do a "last minute" job much later in the tournament. And, since Sven-Goran Eriksson, as a foreigner, is unfit to be knighted, his deputy Steve McClaren should receive a knighthood in his stead - in the field, if necessary. Moreover, this result, and the disparity it exposes, casts grave doubt upon the too-hasty decision to grant Jamaica its independence in 1958. Clearly, it would be better for that island's people to rejoin the Commonwealth so that they might enjoy once again the benefits of subservience to a better and more benevolent ruler - Queen Elizabeth, who is known to take a robustly dim view of "skanking" and all the bad habits into which her former subjects have fallen. Let us replace the reggae dance with the altogether more rational robot dance.

ENGLAND V PARAGUAY (World Cup opening round tie)
June 10, 2006

England labour to victory, hanging on by virtue of a Paraguayan own goal. David Beckham is apparently the victim of an illegal foul from behind.

EXCEPTIONAL ENGLAND ANNIHILATE PERNICIOUS PARAGUAYANS 1-0

In 1982, the British sent a task force to the Falkland Islands to reclaim these precious gems of Empire from the perfidious, swarthy hands of the Argentinean invaders. We went to war for the sake of old maids cycling to evensong, warm beer and so that "sheep might safely graze" upon those isles. It was a defining moment in our history. Many among the international community wished us well in our fight to repel the moustached occupier. Were Paraguay among their number? I believe not. Rather, they laid low and tacit in the long grass of cowardice. We do not forget this lightly.

It is against this seething political backdrop of spineless, ill-advised treachery that the fixture between England and Paraguay took place, the first slab in the paving of England's path to ultimate glory. Now, there are those who, mysteriously, resent Paraguay for having harboured fugitives from the German High Command following World War II. However, that they gave shelter to these staunch, elderly Teutons whose only mistake was to fancy that they could best England in a military scrap does Paraguay a modicum of honour. It is the Paraguayan silence on the Falklands affair that we disciples of St. George cannot forgive.

In truth, this game was won when the flags of the respective nations were first devised. The Cross Of St George, with the colour red streaked like blood from the nose of a foe carved up with a British-made stainless steel knife for his impudence, sets all decent hearts pumping. The Paraguayan flag, by contrast, looks as if they merely adopted the French flag and attached to its middle some kind of crushed spider motif, in the hope that no one would notice their unspeakable vagabondry.

The national anthems again provided proof of the intrinsic superiority of the English. Ours was bellowed with such gusto that they ducked for cover as far away as Dresden. Meanwhile, so absurdly long-winded was the Paraguayan anthem that it is probable that the Presidency of that benighted country changed hands twice during its ponderous rendition.

No doubt, prior to the commencement of the game, emissaries from the English Football Association sent word to the Paraguayan dressing room to offer them a last chance; concede the game to England and there will be no need for your players to come out onto the field and face inevitable humiliation. However, with the arrogance of the Dauphin in the Bard's Henry V, out they trotted regardless, a slap in the face to compound their collaboration in the Falklands affair. It is no wonder, really. Unlike fans of England, whose support for their team is tempered by doughty good humour and native common sense, the Paraguayan people are victims of a collective mania when it comes to their association football prospects. One has read, or at any rate imagined, accounts of the indigenous peoples of Paraguay slaughtering donkeys, even partaking in infant sacrifice in order to placate the footballing gods and attain preferment for their team.

Fortunately, God is an Englishman, as David Beckham proved with a superb early goal, deliberately bounced in off the head of a Paraguayan defender in a comedic touch that drew for its humorous effect on the inherent amusingness of all South Americans. At this rate, a final result of 30-0 could and should have been achieved, were it not for a referee whose suspicious pigmentation should have precluded him from officiating over this fixture. It is an insult to the English that English officials, universally acknowledged as the finest, most fair-minded and most well-groomed in the world, are not allowed to preside in World Cup matches involving the English team. Can we not run our own affairs? Are we to be dictated to by foreigners whose palms have been greased as comprehensively as their hair?

The blatant bias of this referee was most evident when David Beckham found himself the victim of an assault from behind which, in a less lax age, would have seen its perverted perpetrator condemned to several years imprisonment at Reading Gaol. Sodomy, it seems, is no longer a bookable offence.

Come the second half and the Paraguayan team embarked upon a series of unprovoked attacks on the English team. Steven Gerrard in particular replied with warning shots of his own, deliberately aimed high over the bar of the Paraguayan goal when he could easily have fired fatally into the net. Yet even this did not quell their dusky impertinence. After a while, the unspeakable 28-degree heat did take its toll – they were the sort of conditions that prompt otherwise decent Englishmen to sail upriver, declare themselves Village Overlords and impale upon bamboo branches the heads of their grateful native constituents, crying as they do so, "The horror! The horror!" It is a credit to the resilience and restraint of the English team that they did not resort to such tactics.

Eventually, however, the final whistle blew and the Paraguayans were duly bested. This has been an instructive fixture from which two things clearly emerge. The first is that with England in this kind of form - Crouch's aerial dominance, Owen's razor sharpness, Lampard's usefulness, Ashley Cole's sure-footedness, Owen Hargreaves's tactical relevance - FA officials should suggest to their opposite numbers in Brazil, Argentina, Italy, Holland and so forth that they undertake a 'negotiated withdrawal' from this tournament so as to avoid being torn apart by England's strike force.

The second is that, in memory of the Falklands, gunboats currently stationed at those islands should be dispatched to Paraguay forthwith to issue a 21-gun salute, firing randomly onto the coastal towns of that country and their outlying suburbs in celebration. There is one good reason why this cannot be done: Paraguay is landlocked. However, were the Navy to perform this operation along the coastline of Paraguay's near-neighbour Uruguay, in order that they pass on the message, it would amount to the same thing, these South Americans all being much of a muchness when it comes down to common sense brass tacks.

ENGLAND V TRINIDAD & TOBAGO (World Cup opening round tie) June 15, 2006

England leave it very late indeed against unfancied opposition, with Crouch breaking the deadlock, and almost his opponent's dreadlocks, to open the scoring.

INSPIRED ENGLAND TEAR APART TRINIDAD & TOBAGO: 2-0 RESULT FLATTERS CARIBBEANS

In the 1930s, the city of Nuremberg played host to a series of rallies staged by the country's High Command, the spectacle of which mesmerised both German citizens and many of us abroad. However, they were as nothing to the late rally staged by England in this one-sided contest. It was an extraordinary victory for the English, who found themselves having to face not one but two teams, to wit, the combined forces of Trinidad and Tobago. However, John Bull is always at his spunkiest when the odds are against him and so it proved this evening.

In truth, this fixture was won they day the England Band formed in the cobbled backstreets of Sheffield. Their sublime and euphonious brass ensemble playing, the sophistication of which is beyond the grasp of any West Indian, has ensured that England play with the wind at their backs in every game, galvanised to greater heights by the efforts of these musical maestros. The Trinidadians and Tobagans, by contrast, are reduced to bonging out rudimentary tunes on upturned dustbin lids, battered through years of being banged together by these West Indian rascals in street alleys to alert each other when the police are hot on their heels.

Of course, the Trinidadians and Tobagans are a happy, cheerful, smiling people, and so they have proven in this tournament. They were happy, cheerful and smiling at the end of the game, regardless of the result. (The mathematical capability required to keep score is beyond the average West Indian, who would rather fan himself under a tree than attend to his sums, I'd trow!). No doubt, it will be the duty of the British Ambassador on the morrow to explain to his Caribbean counterparts, with the aid of salt and pepperpots, the final tally.

Still, the Trinidadian and Tobagan fans turned out in droves and it was pleasing to see their women dancing, happily, smilingly and cheerfully, in large numbers. What a shame that they did not dance bare-breasted, as that would have made for a still more pleasing, and quite proper, spectacle. We are all used to television documentaries showing the womenfolk of primitive cultures dancing and jiggling vigorously; it could be classified, in this case, as "educational" rather than "disgusting".

From the outset, however, it was clearly England who had the whip-hand, though not literally, to the regret of some. The West Indians cowered in their own penalty box; John Terry in particularly snorted contemptuously, with the look of an old, straw hatted plantation overseer trying to persuade some malfeasant native worker from a coconut tree, the servant clinging desperately to its branches, refusing to shin down and be administered the thrashing that is so clearly his due.

As the game persisted, England at the very least administered a lesson in how the game ought to be played. Gerrard and

Lampard linked up flawlessly, Rio Ferdinand was entirely awake, Michael Owen cobra-like, Beckham unpredictable, Joe Cole's mazy runs leading anywhere but up his own backside. What a pity that, rather than stand respectfully back and admire their skills, as is their place, the Trinidadians and Tobagans chose to resort to impertinent, potentially violent blocking tactics, typical of this happy, smiling, cheerful, sullen, cold-eyed people, no strangers to the machete.

If I would admit to one tiny flaw it was in an effort at goal by the leviathan Peter Crouch, who confounded the Trinidadian and Tobagan defence as if it were confronted with some carved stone god. Rather than opt for the easy tap-in, he attempted a coup de grace that would have made him the toast of the Empire and in so doing, mysteriously lost his footing, with the ball rolling harmlessly towards the corner flag. Since this game was featured on the commercial channel, they saw fit to broadcast a slow motion action replay of the incident, compounding the humiliation of this excellent gentleman. Had the match been transmitted by the British Broadcasting Corporation, they would, I'd warrant, have had the taste to fade discreetly to black and play the national anthem for the offending 10 seconds.

Come the second half and the Trinidadians and Tobagans had the immortal rind to make excursions into the England half, the spectacle of which was deeply offensive to those whose memories extend to those happy years before 1962, when independence was unwisely conferred on this archipelago. Back in those days, a game like this would have presented little anxiety. Any goals scored by the Trinidadians, or Tobagans for that matter, would have instantly become the property of the Crown and therefore added to England's tally. Glad times - 22 men working together for a common aim. However, such is the insolence of the modern age that these dark fellows dared approach the England penalty box, forelocks untugged, as if demanding instant entry to the Garrick Club without having been put up by existing members. Fleetingly, these were anxious times - however, stout Englishman and true kept the faith as they watched, forbearing from shouting at their television sets such remarks as: "You useless, clueless, ponderous, lumpen, overpaid pack of _unts!" Our faith was vindicated with two late but utterly inevitable goals. Send them victorious! Qualification to the knockout phase is guaranteed. Congratulations are due not just to the players, naturally, but to the management and backroom staff. Take a bow, then, Steve McClaren, Sammy Lee, Gary Lewin and Ray Clemence.

A sense of triumph is tempered by indignation that England have to be put through the indignity of the qualifying rounds, which can lead to unnecessary strain on the nerves and acts of insurrection, albeit futile, on the part of our inferiors. Indeed, tomorrow morning, the English Football Association should summon the President of FIFA to its Soho headquarters and put to him an ultimatum. Unless England are given automatic passage to the quarter finals in the 2010 tournament, we shall refuse to participate. Ha! I'd like to see them try to stage a successful World Cup without England! For one thing, they would need to forge a replica trophy as we would refuse to give up the one we shall win this time - a bogus cup to match a bogus and discredited tournament.

I would further recommend that, by way of a permanent reminder of the footballing lesson they were delivered this day, Trinidad & Tobago should agree to our demand that they rename their country Ferdinand & Dorigo, by way of tribute to excellent England footballers past and present. They could, of course, refuse, that is their right. They should consider, however, that were they to do so, they would be placing their cheerful, smiling, happy people, men, women and children, in the gravest peril. Our gunboats are poised; Crouch and Gerrard's strikes should be considered but the opening salvos in a campaign to right recent wrongs.

ENGLAND V SWEDEN (World Cup opening round tie)
June 20, 2006

Once again, England fail to defeat Sweden, whom they have not beaten since 1968, after another indifferent second-half performance, and an injury time lapse in concentration that sees Larsson pull the score back to 2-2.)

EXCELLENT ENGLAND'S BRACE PUTS SORRY SWEDES IN THEIR PLACE*

In the eleventh century, Viking hordes, setting sail from the shores of Sweden, raided and pillaged Scotch coastal villages, having their wicked way with the womenfolk as they plundered. Of course, then as now, the Scotch were valued per head as the equivalent of cattle. Even livestock, however, are part of the Empire and what the odious Swedes visited upon these creatures, subhuman and disloyal as they may be, is an abomination overdue for vengeance.

It could be said that we "shafted" Sweden; I would not resort to such crude and scatological terminology. Suffice it to say, however, that in the first half of this fixture, player by player, we methodically prised apart the Swedes' buttocks, having pulled down their shorts and underpants, paused only to apply the appropriate lubricants and unguents, then thrust, thrust, thrust, thrust, thrust, thrust, thrust, thrust, thrust, thrust, thrust, thrust and thrust again, until the Swedes themselves appeared in certain cases to enjoy the intensity of the chastisement they were suffering. Each Englishman took his turn with his opposite number, as schoolboys in the crowd threw their caps in the air in appreciation of the spectacle. Buggery remains a crime which in a more proper age would, when practised by homosexuals, be punishable by castration and indefinite imprisonment. However, as with certain initiation ceremonies at our public schools and

Freemasons' lodges, there are times when buggery is a patriotic imperative on the part of normal young Englishmen. This was just such an occasion.

In truth, this fixture was morally won the first time an Englishman bought a flat-pack from IKEA, discovered a vital screw to be missing, then smashed the unassembled pieces of wood to smithereens before instructing his wife to gather together the wreckage into a carrier bag and make the 40 minute bus ride to the nearest IKEA branch to demand a refund. The Swedish as a team, as a nation, have a key component missing - they are not English - and it was this England sought to put to their advantage. Hence a first half display which will have the likes of Spain and Argentina scurrying comically about in panic as if pursued by angry bulls bent on goring their hindquarters, with England showing how the game should be played: directly, unimpeded, with foreigners sullenly and cluelessly accepting their inferior lot.

Come the second half, however, and the true, insidious nature of the Swedish nation revealed itself in all its blue and yellow revoltingness. From their stubborn refusal to assist us militarily against Iceland in the Cod Wars, the Swedes have engaged in a campaign of low-level subversiveness against the English. They have distracted our men with their au pairs, reduced our man hours of productiveness with their online pornography, confused and depressed us with their plays, films and half-time team talks. Yes, on this matter one can no longer remain silent: the Swedes somehow installed one of their own as manager of our very own team. One could compare this to appointing Hermann Goering as head of the RAF during the Second World War; except that Eriksson's appointment is far, far worse.

Still, England's yeomen overcame this Quisling impediment and played like men possessed in the second half; possessed of everything but the ball, one might concede, but our cocks did not wilt after Mellberg, unfairly converting a chance with his beard (memo to FIFA, please ensure that all goals scored by players sporting facial hair be deemed inadmissible, with previous results revised accordingly), restored parity. Thankfully, England's frontline, led by Peter "The Option" Crouch were unfazed by this freak occurrence and sanity was restored with a pinpoint header from Steven Gerrard, who, if you took out a dagger and made a St George's cross on his chest. would bleed English red. Why has nobody yet done so? Political correctness, perhaps?

Mentioned in dispatches is Sol Campbell whose entry onto the pitch inspired a confidence reminiscent of silent movies when the Keystone Cops came tearing round the corner. And so it proved when in the later stages he came within a yard of leaping to prevent what would have been a Swedish equaliser.

I learn from my manservant Seppings that the latest talk is of Argentina being favourites - this despite the biffing we gave them in 1982. In order to quell such talk (for which Seppings tasted the stinging end of my riding crop) it seems more urgent than ever to men of sentience that the 2006 World Cup should be awarded, in advance, to England. FIFA might quibble but no matter; the SAS should abseil in and smoke bomb their way into FIFA's headquarters to seize the trophy, which could then be presented to the English team, helicoptered en masse overnight to the lawns of Buckingham Palace, so that the surprise ceremony should not take place on foreign soil.

It is imperative too, in this time of global conflict, that the press be subject to censorship in order to keep English spirits up and that a body be set up to vet all World Cup Reports to ensure that they are not riddled with information which might sap national morale.

Finally, it's clear that Sweden, for their multitude of sins against the English, deserve to be taught a lesson. Here is my suggestion. Raids, hundreds of them, across every English city, on every property harbouring a Swedish au pair, ambassador, meatball roller or herring pickler. Load them onto trucks, then herd them into a branch of IKEA burned out and gutted by the British Army in advance. Lock the doors behind them, seal up the windows, then fill the premises with gas. Of course, it would be harmless laughing gas and they would emerge chuckling helplessly at the British sense of humour. However, if a few canisters should get mixed up, or if a few Swedes are trampled to death or suffer heart attacks in the ensuing panic, we are certainly not to be blamed for any deficiency in the Scandinavian sense of irony.

*Headline passed by the Provisional Board Of English World Cup Censors

ENGLAND V ECUADOR (World Cup second round)
June 25, 2006

England qualify for the quarter-finals as David Beckham recovers from illness brought on by heat exhaustion to score the decisive goal. Meanwhile, John Terry makes another uncustomary defensive error.

AWESOME ENGLAND VOMIT UPON ECUADOR FROM A GREAT HEIGHT 1-0

In my youth, I spent many months among the indigenous peoples of Ecuador. If I had expected hostility, I was to be surprised. They invited me into their homes, bade me share their meals, and evidently regarded me as one of their own. I soon put them straight. I had several of the savages build me a house high in the trees of the forest, from whence I would take potshots with my blunderbuss at any of the natives persistent enough to approach me with one of their ghastly pots of banana stew. A more backward, leaf-chewing, goat-slaughtering shower you could not hope or wish to meet, and overly familiar to boot. The purposes of my visit to Ecuador were commercial not fraternal, as I was obliged to convey to one or two of them with the steel-tipped end of my stick.

It was against this backdrop of staggering impudence in regarding themselves the equals of Englishmen that this second round match took place. In truth, this fixture was won the day half a dozen seasick Spaniards arrived by boat and duly took over the entire country of Ecuador. Such is the dominance of the European mindset over the South American that David Beckham, green with nausea and hurling up his guts, doubtless beset with feverish hallucinations, could nonetheless find it within himself to unleash the decisive shot, like a brigadier firing his revolver to quell restive locals. He showed them what English stomachs are made of.

The game began with the Ecuadorians engaging in typical South American cynical tactics: communicating with each other in a jabbering code of their own devising rather than plain, comprehensible English. Not like our own Mr Beckham, whose every move was telegraphed without cowardly obfuscation. Each time he shaped up, he was saying, "Now see here, you dusky rabble. I am about to launch the ball, with my foot, high and true in the general direction of your penalty area. Stand by to be confounded by my technique. That is all."

England exhibited patience, waiting for an opening, though they need only have waited for a plane to pass overhead, at which point the Ecuadorians would doubtless have fallen to the ground in worshipful abasement, imagining it to be a Sky God of some sort. Air traffic must have been scarce, however, for it was the Ecuadorians who took advantage of a momentary stillness on the part of John Terry - he could be forgiven for taking time out to pose, in his imagination, for the statue which will surely be erected in his honour upon his return home. Thankfully, Ashley Cole, who would quite literally take a bullet in the head if it would prevent a corner to the opposition, threw himself in the way of the oncoming foe.

England were superlative, every man-jack of them. Paul Robinson never looked like he was having such a calamitous day that at any point, his shorts might fall down as he was taking a goal kick, prompting him to trip over his own feet, tumble over and send the ball feebly trickling into his own net. Frank Lampard put in another command performance whose majesty words alone could not convey, least of all the words "utter rubbish".

As the afternoon wore on, the referee, whose car boot should have been checked afterwards lest it contained a crate of bananas bearing the word "gracias", dared to book one or two of our heroic boys for "time-wasting". In truth, he should have booked all eleven of the Ecuadorian team for wasting our time in turning up for this fixture at all, obliging Englanders to spend 90 minutes witnessing what FIFA ought to have marked down as a foregone conclusion and therefore a "bye". The referee even ignored England pleas as players such as Gerrard fell to ground; an unpardonable slight upon our honour. Foreign referees should note that when an Englishman falls to the ground, that is all the information he needs. The matter is settled. A foul must be awarded.

It could be said that the Ecuadorians played the last half hour of this game as if, were they to progress, the cost of the extra hotel bills would bankrupt their national economy. Not so. It was England's defensive impenetrability and attacking acuity which made them wilt. Small wonder that England's next potential opponents, the Portuguese and the Dutch, conspired to get as many of themselves sent off as possible so that they would be ineligible for next Saturday's humiliation. The very thought of John Terry, granite of jaw and strong of thigh, thwacking his hand with a riding crop, is stimulating for some but not for the Portuguese, who will already be ruing their Pyrhhic victory.

No doubt Mr Eriksson has his own ideas as to how to deal

with Portugal in the next round but, since he is Swedish-born, these thoughts are of no consequence. English colleagues such as Sammy Lee should overrule him and determine that next week's quarter-final be used as a chance to rest our first eleven and give a runout to five or six of the players who have seen little action: Walcott, Downing, James, and so forth. Just five or six reserves, playing a 2-1-2 formation, will suffice against the crying women of Portugal. No point in working up an undue sweat.

As for Ecuador, their daring to turn up for this game at all is a slight to add to a greater historical one. During the 19th century, there was an implicit invitation to any nation to join the British Empire voluntarily, putting their natural mineral resources at the disposal of Queen Victoria and the running of their affairs in the hands of British civil servants and farsighted London businessmen. We shall make them regret that they refused to take advantage of this offer. I suggest a 1000 strong squadron of aircraft, advancing and darkening the Ecuadorian skies, spear-headed by the Red Arrows, in wave after wave. From high, they shall, at the signal from their own Wing Commander, drop thousands upon thousands of gallons of white and red paint from the bomb bay doors onto a pre-designated area of rainforest. At a stroke, hitherto superfluous foliage will be converted into a vast, rectangular representation of the St.George flag, one visible from outer space. Granted, one or two tribes might get a bit of a drenching, but that is entirely their fault for refusing to remove those singularly ridiculous things from their lips and join Civilisation and all its attendant benefits and sensibleness.

ENGLAND V PORTUGAL (World Cup quarter final)
July 1, 2006

History repeats itself. Just as in 2004, England are knocked out of a major competition by Portugal, after performing especially poorly in the penalty shootout.

BLAST, BLAST, BLAST, BLAST, BLAST, BLAST, BLAST . . . .

In April 1974, in Portugal, a revolutionary song was broadcast on national radio which triggered the overthrow of the fascist Salazar regime. In what became known as the "carnation revolution", insurgent members of the populace bore flowers to indicate their non-violent intentions towards the military. And so it was that a coup d'état was effected with virtually no blood shed, with Portugal entering a modern era of liberal democracy practically overnight. What a dark day this was for Portugal, for Europe as a whole. It spoke volumes for the fundamental shabbiness of the Portuguese people when they cast off the firm hand of authority, presuming, like monkeys at a zoo who in their mischief have somehow got their claws on the keeper's keys, that they could let themselves loose from their cages of propriety and bound about at large.

It is against this backdrop of staggering disdain for the hierarchical order of peoples that this fixture took place. What, after all, can be said about the Portuguese, this nation of conniving, lawless blackguards whose aspect suggests that they bathe daily in olive oil, whose idea of a sensible breakfast is not the norm of bacon, fried eggs, fried sausages, baked beans, fried hash brown potatoes, black pudding, faggots, fried field mushrooms, bread and dripping, toast and fried marmalade - but a bowl of figs? Figs, I'll warrant, marinated in one of their filthy, fortified wines for which the Portuguese are infamous, which a man would have to fortify himself with several pints of plain English mead before imbibing.

The Portuguese have, of course, met England very recently - in 1966. It was then that they brought to these shores Eusebio, one of the very first negroes. While this was amusing in certain respects, I felt it was a dangerous act of importation. Think of the havoc wrought in the outback when non-indigenous frogs were introduced to that country . . . happily, we tanned their backsides for them and sent them and their "wild man" back home to minimise the risk of erosion to our social fabric.

As the teams lined up in the tunnel, the streets of England fell silent, save for women shopping and homosexuals chalking out the squares for "hopscotch" on deserted pavements, knowing that no men were around to rag them for their disgusting effeminacy. The English, as ever, were paradigms of manhood, hewn from the granite that lies beneath our native soil. The Portuguese, by contrast, with their hair bands and their skins moisturised by excessive crying to referees, were little more than a farrago of perfidious girl-men. The last time I read, homosexuals were not allowed to play Association Football, lest they pass on their condition to other players while jostling at set pieces. I rather suspect that the Portuguese, for reasons of necessity given their stock, were harbouring several homosexuals among their number. There should have been but one way to flush them out. Before the game, the FA should have had a naked John Terry parade up and down in the Portuguese dressing room, with a FIFA representative, superintended by a member of the FA, manually checking the Portuguese players' shorts for suspicious signs of tumescence.

The game commenced and England at once established their dominance. This was not manifested in such vulgar, eager-to-please measures as shots on goal or monopoly of possession. It was enough that they were English, lips curled, looking on at the Southern European foe as he scampered about playing his fancy tricks. So evident was England's innate dominance, personified by the erect carriage and upright bearing of Mr Beckham, that the referee should have stopped the game at half time and awarded it to the team in white, they having built up an unassailable lead in breeding. But then, what are we to expect when FIFA, in their astounding obtuseness, appoint an Argentine referee? A man whose last acquaintance with the English was running across Goose Green with his trousers on fire, screaming for his Mother? If a foreigner must be chosen to officiate, there can be only one acceptable choice: the Duke Of Edinburgh.

Still, England held sway - Joe "chirpy cocksparrer" Cole so entertained his fellow players with his twinkled-toed sideshow that, had he put a cigarette tin at his feet, I would have gladly thrown in tuppence. Frank Lampard proved, once again, that he is as vital to England as is the monarchy. David Beckham, meanwhile, adopted the World War I policy of bombardment and slow attrition. At corners and set pieces, he deliberately pounded the ball against the heads of the first defenders, knowing that before long they would eventually duck rather than take further punishment. Wayne Rooney, as English as a King Edward potato and almost as handsome, threw himself into the fray with blood and gusto, only to fall victim to one of the most unjust and inexplicable refereeing decisions ever made, for which the citizens of Buenos Aires shall be made to pay, once Trident is renewed. If an Englishman cannot stamp hard on the testicles of another man as he lies prostrate without being made to feel that he has somehow done something wrong, then how on earth are we to maintain discipline among our errant servants? Rooney's dismissal strikes a blow to the class system mandated by God himself far harder than any Portuguese testicle has ever suffered.

It was at this point that I made a momentous decision: I decided to remove the tablecloth from my television set (a Scotch invention whose integrity therefore cannot be trusted) and watch the game for myself. Hitherto, my reports have come from two sources: the first editions of the Daily Telegraph, the true newspaper of record, and the accounts of my faithful, 86-year-old retainer Seppings, who scurries up and down the three flights of stairs from the servants' quarters to my study to convey to me news of the game's progress every five minutes. As I watched the remainder of the game unfold with my own eyes, things became very clear.

With David Beckham and Wayne Rooney removed from the field of play, England were reduced to an ignominious shower. At last, one could see in plain sight what many have being saying for some time: that this England team has had no earthly chance of winning the World Cup, and that it was sheer, sanguine folly to imagine otherwise. Owen Hargreaves, a German, perversely, ran about the pitch in a state of desperate panic, as if being pursued by Corporal Jones and his bayonet. Steven Gerrard, whom I learn from Seppings is a "Scouser", ran about as if fleeing the scene of a crime, the crime in his case being that any man who cannot speak the Queen's English without showering all and sundry with coarse, Liverpudlian spittle has no business pulling on an England shirt. He should be put on the next boat to Ireland. That he took his penalty as if meekly returning a stolen football back to its rightful owner, with a constable stood over him ready to fetch him another clip around the ear, is no mitigation.

Finally, there are the cases of "Rio Ferdinand", "Ashley Cole" and "Aaron Lennon". When I at last clapped eyes upon them, well, I - I had been given to believe that . . . to think that all along, I had imagined they were . . . dear, God, to think that they may have shared a shower with the likes of John Terry . . . as I spluttered and gasped, turning first red, then purple, then blue, I could emit but one word: "EEUSEBIO!!!!"

Of course, as was fully to be expected, England are out. The fact that the winning penalty was scored by Ronaldo, a player from the English Premier League, a man playing for an English team, with English teammates, living in an English house with an English garden, eating English food, sleeping in an English bed with an English mattress does, of course, mean that ultimately England won the game. However, this seems of little consolation in this time of disappointment. In truth, this fixture was lost in 1846, the year Parliament repealed the Corn Laws, thereby handing this once-great nation into the hands of a newly enfranchised Plebeian rabble. Hence results like this. England, I was loyal to you; now, I disown you, rank country condemned to progress no further than quarter-finals, your blood and stock weakened by years of interbreeding among inferior classes and races. I renounce my citizenship and pledge my loyalty to Germany, a proud people who had a dream once, which might come to pass yet again. Frau Merkel, I beseech you directly. If you find yourself in the need of a good man and true, not German-born but rabidly loyal to the Fatherland, who could be of some service, perhaps transmitting propaganda messages across the North Sea by mediumwave radio, calculated to sap English morale and reduce her prospects further as a footballer or trading competitor, then you need only say the word. Over and 'raus!

HUGH McLAUGHTON,
BROADSHEET CORRESPONDENT

WHITHER THE MEN OF GRIT HEWN
FROM THE IRONSTONE OF YORE?

Contemplating the primped popinjays, the prancing, petulant powder puffs and protected pansies who pass for the prime of the Premier League nowadays, I am compelled to cast my mind to a better, nobler, truer, grittier, more altogether Caledonian footballing era. This was not so much an Age of Gold, as the French in their unblushing effeminacy would have it, but more an Age of Stone.

For time was, dear reader – I speak, lest you wonder, of the era of such rough-hewn titans as Shankly, Busby, even Ferguson (the senior) - when footballing men were made of more obdurate, impervious stuff. These were men, literally – and I use that oft-overused word in its literal sense – made of granite. They were not born, weak of flesh from their mothers' soft, nether regions like so many of today's pampered youth apprentices, but mined from the true earth, from seams once rich with character and endurance.

In this age of microphones, "soundbites" and colour photo supplements, a transcript of an interview conducted with the legendary Willie Auchtermuchty, the unsung contemporary of Bill Shankly, back in 1938 on BBC radio, speaks volumes in its terseness.

THE BBC: So, Willie, today's the big day, Dunfermline's first appearance in an Association Football Cup Final. I expect you and your team are looking forward to putting on a grand show?

AUCHTERMUCHTY: Aye, laddie.

THE BBC: It seems that the people of Dunfermline have put out the bunting on your behalf. That must rather buck you up?

AUCHTERMUCHTY: Aye, laddie.

THE BBC: Is there anything else you'd care to say to listeners to the British Broadcasting Corporation?

AUCHTERMUCHTY: Aye, laddie.

THE BBC (following a lengthy silence): And what might that be?

AUCHTERMUCHTY: Aye, laddie.

In those few, laconic words was etched the wisdom and accumulated anguish of decades of hardship, hard lives, hard men, hard luck and hard tackling – qualities a Didier Drogba would never understand even if they were thudded hard into his groin with some old fashioned piston device, operated by strong, silent men in cloth caps working for 3d a day. Auchtermuchty's early retirement was brought on following the loss of his left leg after a firm but manful challenge from his lifelong friend and Best Man Jock McMulty – according to legend, McMulty personally handed him back his severed, bleeding limb in the centre circle as they exchanged brisk handshakes at the end of the game. Substitutions were properly considered the provenance of netball in those manlier, Scottisher times, so Auchtermuchty struggled on with just his functioning right leg, setting up two goals in the second half in a thrilling 9-7 encounter. There was honour among men, blood both spilt and shared.

Where am I going with all this? Back into the mists of time, where the pansyish Portuguese, the footling French and the ginger Germans of whom today's "Premiership" so shamefully consists, fear to tread for damaging their Nike-sponsored soles in the true grit of authenticity. The times when men, lived, breathed and ate football. Again, literally, in the 30s, when even haggis was scarce and all that a family had to subsist upon was the leather ball that had earlier in the Sabbath been booted against a tenement wall, with the bairns vying for the slice that included the bootlace, considered, erroneously, to be made of liquorice.

One thinks of Tom Finney, who eschewed the cigarette break at half time during internationals (this is to say, the half time break from cigarettes, which were smoked freely on the pitch during the 90 minutes in those more "politically incorrect" times) in order to run out of the Empire Stadium into the two-up, two down terracing opposite the ground to earn his keep with a quick plumbing job, in full kit, cash in hand, before returning onto the pitch to slam four past the overrated, and admittedly seasick European opposition to make the final tally 9-6. If Tom Finney were to hear of footballers earning their stipend exclusively from the playing of the game rather than learning a trade as electrician, slaughterman, tinker or victualler, he would turn in his grave. And yes, reader, before you set fountain pen to paper, I should point out that I realise Tom is alive and well and probably more than capable of turning out for his country. I merely venture to suggest that he would be so disgusted, he would go out, dig his own grave and lie in it, turning the way he used to turn defenders, in order to make his point. He is that sort of man, the sort England, in its effete folly, no longer welds or manufactures.

These were the days of Stanley Matthews, who, even at the age of 56 and still a top-flight player for Stoke City, spurned the holidays in France and Spain partaken by the fashionable "longhairs", ruined by the profligacy of 25 guineas a week wages. As was his wont since the 30s, he and his family took camping holidays in the Peak District, using two pairs of his own adequately voluminous shorts as tents, rented from the club at the rate of a shilling and fourpence a week, or a shilling and twopence in off season, from the club's benevolent billionaire owners The Potter Brothers. Try telling that to the likes of a Craig Bellamy and they would laugh at you like a woman at a hen party, and wrongly so.

One thinks again of the legendary "Auld Firm" clashes, in which crowds of 295,000 would regularly turn out to watch Celtic and Rangers hammer out their respective claims to local pre-eminence. Sixty or seventy spectators would die during these fixtures on a weekly basis, not of stadium collapse, as became the fashion in the foppish 1980s but of natural causes. The life expectancy among the tenants of the Gorbals was not high. A truly hard man could not expect to live beyond the age of 27. Such sense of community laid the basis for the "Lisbon Lions" -

the first team ever to win the European Cup whose eleven members were of such close proximity, to the extent that they shared the same bed. Hotels in Portugal were not cheap in 1967, though doubtless Mr (Mrs?) Mourinho would be confounded by the gritty economic realities of his forbears.

And so, back to Willie Auchtermuchty, retired at 26, due to limb loss. He was swiftly appointed manager of Dunfermline, and become mentor to the legendary Allie McMeoch, the "Flying Scotsman" who had an eye for the ladies. Auchtermuchty took swift action. Taking advantage of a loophole in a Scottish by-law, he divorced his own wife and took Mr McMeoch as his second spouse, with a view to preserving his footballing energies from the loin-sapping wiles of the female populace. Would a Mourinho consider doing the same for a Ballack? One jeeringly suspects not. That the Auchtermuchty-McMeoch marriage produced seven children, all strong boys as befits such a masculine coupling, speaks further volumes about the age, an age, then as now, when We Were Men and Europeans Were Women.

ENGLAND V GREECE (Friendly)
August 16, 2006

England take apart the surprise winners of Euro 2004 – the promise of the great things to come under new manager Steve McClaren.

ASTONISHING ENGLAND REGAIN COMMAND OF FOOTBALL'S HIGH SEAS AS GREECE LOSE MARBLES 4-0

Some 2,200 years ago, the Greek thinker Archimedes lowered himself into a bath. Only moments later, he would be struck by an epiphany which would prove a turning point in the thinking of his countrymen; with a demented shriek he at once leapt from his tub and ran naked down the street. For, in that moment he had realised that no Greek man, nor indeed any Southern European, could commit himself to so hygienic an act as to immerse himself in soapy water. Hence, since that day, the Greeks have carried with them the stench of overcooked aubergines, the sun-dried corpses of slaughtered livestock and "wines" that make their moustached, idle citizenry walking magnets for roaming, aniseed-fixated packs of mangy stray dogs.

The Greeks were similarly out of their element as they faced up to England on the battlefield of Old Trafford last night. These men had the haunted look of a team already crushed by the weight of historical inevitability. Their national anthem was less a proud call to arms, more of a craven, widow's plea for mercy in the face of the foe. It cut no ice with the proud forces of the axis nations in World War II, nor did it tonight.

England played in white; their shirts, however, appeared red, soaked as they were in a vat of English blood, to which each squad member contributed a pint at the insistence of new manager, Steven "Steve" McClaren, whose ruddy capillaries suggested he had squeezed out half a pint himself. John Terry was at the helm, yodelling the English national anthem so lustily it could be heard across the English channel, with French villagers running around ringing church bells in fear. "Long live our Noble Queen!" he bellowed. He could easily have been referring to himself, for John Terry is noble indeed. Just the man you'd want next to you in the trenches, where men are packed together like sardines, writhing in the mud, caught up in the passion and thrust of the fray.

As for the Greeks, here is a nation whose contributions to civilisation you can count on the fingers of one hand: urns, homosexuality, cheap men's hair dye as advertised in the pages of periodicals such as the Daily Express, and crockery abuse. The English, by contrast, have contributed to the world Philosophy, and it is a philosophy that runs as follows: "Run! Run! Run your guts out! Get in there! Knock it with passion! Up! Upfield! Heart!

Ferdinand to Crouch! Passion! Guts! Trenches! Kick it! Kick it away, kick it away! Run! Through walls, heart first! Throw it up! Throw up! Blood in the trenches! Fire! Fire! Don't panic! Don't panic!!" As the Greeks cravenly strung series after series of passes together, as if threading together fishing nets rather than playing association football, it became clear that they, like their fellow Europeans, were sadly lacking in any comprehension of this philosophy.

Inevitably, it was not long before England, playing with their guts on fire, began to run up a tally of goals, with the Greek defence looking on idly from a distance, like members of their own police force as a man is robbed, beaten and buggered to death in broad daylight, right under their noses on the harbour front, as they masticate kebab. Gary Neville, with his little moustache, worked the channel like a tugboatman going back and forth to Dunkirk. Jermain Defoe evaded the Greek offside trap with great cunning, only being caught out about 37 times per half, rendering the words "gormless" and "dozy" and "silly little twat" utterly obsolete. Frank Lampard showed that the adage that the mark of a great referee is that you barely notice he's on the pitch can equally be applied to players. John Terry, so erect and engorged with blood in the heat of the tussle was, he will not mind my saying, half man, half penis.

By half time, the game was up; the silence of unsmashed saucers from the Greek dressing room was deafening. In the second half, the Greeks staged a counter-attack, but had they trundled into the penalty box in a wooden box, their attacking ploy could not have been more predictable. England toyed with them, teased them, particularly the lofty Peter Crouch, playing as if dangling our Elgin Marbles before them, then pulling them up, out of reach - "Ah, ah, ah! Finders, keepers!" - as their little men leapt up and tried to snatch them from his grasp. At last, the final whistle blew, and it was a long, long ferry ride home for the Greeks, down Manchester canal, then round this sceptr'd isle, with their players ruing their over-indulgence in moussaka as the bracing English seas buffeted their rusty, floating urinal of a vessel.

This result, naturally, makes an anomalous laughing stock of the recent World Cup. It is for FIFA to decide whether to recall the cup from Rome and have it retrospectively awarded to England on the strength of last night's performance. However, history will judge them to be knaves and foreign fools if they do not. As for Man Of The Match Owen Hargreaves, let us not procrastinate longer: hand-picked members of the SAS must be dispatched to Munich this very night, to scale the walls of the Bayern stadium where he is held captive (though doubtless, being English, he has been digging a tunnel under the pitch to Switzerland for months now) and spirit him back to England, leaving a trail of German corpses in their wake.

And so, having bested the European Champions, England can now add the title of European Champions themselves to their impressive list of footballing spoils, as well as to our marbles. The Greek ambassador shall be summoned to the FA this morning, with the trophy; if he fails to turn up, his nation shall face the consequences; and, believe me, unlike the Italians, we shall come armed with more than just mandolins.

ENGLAND V ANDORRA (European Championship qualifier)
September 2, 2006

England crush the tiny principality in their opening qualifier for Euro 2008. They simply cannot stop winning under manager McClaren, notwithstanding a further uncharacteristic error by John Terry.

ELEGANT ENGLAND SWEEP ASIDE DANGEROUS, MAN-EATING MINNOWS OF ANDORRA 5-0

Despite the nine million tourists who visit the principality-cum-hamlet each year, very, very little is known, not even by myself, of Andorra, which lies in an unhappy geographical position between Spain and France in the Pyrenees. Therefore one can only conjecture on the country's history and background, based on close examination of the overtanned complexions and countenances of its association footballers, who lined up against England's stalwart lions, mouth-breathing their national anthem which was evidently composed for Jew's harp and two water jugs. Here, then, are the facts as I take them.

- It is thought that the country is led by a Grand Sorcerer, half man, half goat, who dwells on Andorra's highest peak and can turn men into tree-frogs if they provoke his ire.

- The entire population of Andorra could be crushed into the back of a large juggernaut; as indeed they were, in order to take up their full ticket allocation, journeying arduously to Manchester via France, Italy, Romania, Greece, then across the seas to Portugal, before alighting eventually at Liverpool. Fortunately, the Andorran mountain peoples, who live on average to be 137, can go months without food, water, even port.

- Football was only introduced to Andorra in 1996 by a FIFA emissary who travelled to the principality on donkey-back. The visit was not auspicious. He was forced to flee, under a hail of blowdarts from the hostile locals; moreover, when presented with the football he had brought them, the Andorrans promptly ate it.

It was against such a people - comical, queer, amusingly unnumerous, mostly called Sanchez, dangerous, filthy mountain bandits led by a mad sorcerer, that England's boys were ranged. This had the makings of a difficult game. Wes Brown in particular, who has about him the look of some sort of botched experiment, already looked as if he might have caught the wrath of The Sorcerer.

Soon, however, England were in the ascendancy, as Peter Crouch, giraffe-like in his predatory aggression, opened the scoring. The tension, hitherto unbearable, was broken as Britannia had once more defied both the foreigner and the odds. The Sanchezes looked at one another in confusion, their movements perhaps impeded by having to wear lace-up boots rather than play barefoot; their little left-back, who was in constant danger of being substituted and replaced by his own mother, was no match for Steven Gerrard who showed once again than when allowed the time, space and deference that is his due from foreigners, he will play with distinction. The Portuguese in particular would do well to pay heed to the Andorran defence's properly respectful attitude towards England's second greatest Englishman.

The extent of England's achievement is all the more staggering given that this was by no means a full-strength English team; no Neville, no Rooney, no Ferdinand, no Cole, no Owen, no Beckham, no Charlton, no Moore, no Finney. Yet so laughable were Andorra's attempts to surge forward that England could almost have afforded to play David James in goal. As it was, they allowed Phil Neville a run-out, the footballing equivalent of when The Beatles allowed their drummer, Richard "Ringo" Starr, to play and perform one or two songs on their inexplicably popular phonographs.

There were outstanding performances across the park: from Defoe and Hargreaves, as well as Ashley Cole - Cool, Unflappable, Nonchalant, Towering - I sense a new nickname for the man in the offing. However, it was two other Chelsea stalwarts who stole the day with typically dominant displays. Frank Lampard took the stadium's breath away with one free kick from 20 yards out, which, had the Andorran goalkeeper not made a lucky interception, would have come rolling to a stand-still a mere foot or two from the goal-line. Exquisite. Then, of course, there was John "The Thighs" Terry. His attempt to convert the ball into an unguarded net from six inches out, in which he very nearly headed the ball out of the stadium, is testament to his extraordinary properties.

Though it is properly said of England that there are no difficult fixtures at this level, perhaps there was a kernel of truth in the remarks of one of the English commentators that there are certain teams, the very minnows and insignificant anchovies of European football, who should perhaps play in groups among themselves before presuming to trouble Europe's giants, sleeping or otherwise: Andorra, Liechtenstein, Luxembourg, The Faroe Islands, San Marino, The Isle Of Man, Gibraltar, Rockall, Lundy, the lighthouse off Beachy Head, Northern Ireland, Wales.

That said, following this disgracefully inadequate performance, the authorities should see to it that Andorra, as a "nation", should be relegated from Europe, to Asia. If they fail to prove themselves even in that lesser continent, they should be demoted further down, to Africa, and so forth until finally they languish in Oceania. Glory and power to the strong and numerous, ruin and humiliation to the tiny and sparse. And now to the scullery, to seek out the small boy who comes in every other Tuesday to clean my boots and knives, and rain blows upon his feeble frame with my whangee cane.

ENGLAND V MACEDONIA (European Championship qualifier) September 6, 2006

England edge past Macedonia thanks to a goal by Peter Crouch, who is then substituted for much-touted England star in waiting, the hairless Andrew Johnson. Ashley Cole is booked in the 89th minute for timewasting.

INCOMPARABLE ENGLAND SPANK MACEDONIAN HIDES RED RAW 1-0

"Mcdnian! Rrnt noci rrbi yyet!

"Hja hja flvvip!

"Vaci Vaci tyci wrn!

Soup!"

The above is an extract, rendered phonetically, of the Macedonian national anthem. It translates as: "Macedonian men! Open thy perfumed thighs! Wrestle with the foe as the bald eagle does laugh aloud at the girlish warthog! Then celebrations! Celebrations! Pomegranates, jumping, men dressed as antelopes! The women are grubby, dirty! Men! Men! Men! Men! Men! And soup."

Such were our opponents. Macedonia's history is a turbulent one: an extraneous Balkan appendix, a vowel-starved hell-hole whose national flag looks like some sort of Kamikaze headband. Most famously, Macedonia was birthplace to Alexander The Great, the world's first homosexual (the second was Quentin Crisp). There is no confusion about this. This was perhaps England's most pernicious foe: Macedonia, the cradle of sodomy, in whose national genes rabid ambitions for global domination still rage. Still, England's darkest hour has often been its finest, and so again it proved tonight.

Thankfully, the Macedonians are an absolute shambles of a people. During the performance of the national anthems, members of the Republic Of Macedonia Army could clearly be seen shooing livestock off the pitch in the background. The two teams lined up, each with a row of boys from the opposing team in front of them. From the swarthy, leery expressions creased into the faces of the Macedonian players, it was clear that, raging Alexandrians to a man, they were under the impression that these English boys were presents of some sort, to be taken home and disposed of according to their pleasure. Perhaps they considered the shaven-headed urchins arranged in front of the England team as fair exchange. What can one say about such a team? One can only wonder what process of fertilisation, what implements and utensils were employed to bring them into this world, with their neglected womenfolk playing a mere surgical role in the necessary business of procreation.

At last, the game began. And, with the Macedonians signally failing to fall into the proper foreign formation of Guard Of Honour, as performed by the Andorrans, England found themselves impeded, unable to play their natural game which, at its most graceful and sublime, requires the absence of any opposition at all. The pitch, veritably Balkan in its topography, was a hindrance; time and again, England's attacking flow was broken up as they found themselves tripping over cowpats, Kosovan landmines, the shallow graves of dissidents, and so forth.

Soon, however, England were in the ascendancy. Hargreaves continues to get more English by the game. Stuart Downing ran up and down the left flank so effectively that it ought hereafter to be paved and renamed "Downing Street", with a British bobby permanently standing guard thereupon. As for Frank Lampard, it was enough that he was, simply, Frank Lampard - yet another triumph of "being" over "doing". Steven Gerrard would have been immense were it not for his being tackled on several occasions by players of inferior pedigree in what can only be described as a gross breach of international protocol. Small wonder that he stood, hands on hips, breathing hard and staring with exasperation as if to say, "Do you know who I am?" Macedonia's ambassador will be required to explain himself this morning.

All of this cut little ice with the referee, a Frenchman. With the Napoleonic Wars still fresh in the minds of many of us, this was a crass decision by FIFA. Doubtless, England's representatives only agreed to his appointment on condition that he be made to wear an appropriately yellow shirt. However, such was his incli-nation towards the Macedonians, that even when one of of their defenders attempted to wrestle Peter Crouch and strip him to his undershorts, he pooh-poohed protests, as if to suggest that Crouch should have been flattered. For this perfidy alone, FIFA should have insisted that the referee emerge in the second half in a pink wig and can-can dancer's knickerbockers.

England emerged triumphant in the second half, however, with Crouch blasting home from Lampard's perfectly weighted and judged miskick. At this point, a twin-bladed Sikorski military helicopter should have descended onto the pitch, thrown out a rope ladder and winched the England team up and out of that benighted stadium back to Civilisation, with the game declared won. Astonishingly, however, the referee insisted that the match continue, with the result that Macedonia almost grabbed an equaliser, which would have been a Balkan outrage to match the assassination of the Archduke Franz Ferdinand. Thankfully, Ashley Cole was on the line to demonstrate an equal capability with both left and right feet. Finally, Andy "Andrew" Johnson took to the field, reflecting, doubtless, on his luck to be an Englishman. Had he been born a Macedonian, he would almost certainly be wheeled from village to village in a wooden cage, billed as "The Human Egg-Man", with peasants paying three ploddynks for a glance at his remarkable cranium.

Of course, it sticks like a foreign pickle in the craw that England, once again setting the footballing Gold Standard by which all foreigners should measure their inferiority, were obliged to play against a country which, historians concur, ceased to exist many centuries ago. Who might we next be asked to play? Assyria? Gaul? Hibernia? Mesopotamia?

For its part, however, Macedonia has borne witness to a new hero, to displace Alexander The Great. I refer, of course, to Terry The Great. For many months now, I have been working on a frieze, some 30 feet by 60 feet, depicting a naked John Terry, head jutted triumphantly aloft, wearing a helmet as worn by the warriors of ancient yore, a chorus of young boys kneeling at his feet, looking up adoringly and enviously. The image is drawn both from photographs and sketches of Master Terry, a collection of which I keep in my potting shed, while in certain particulars I have resorted to my imagination. I propose to lend the frieze to the Macedonian embassy, so that they may replicate as the centrepiece for a newly minted coat of arms. Thereafter, I propose to wheel it to Stamford Bridge and make a present of it to the cockneys of Chelsea Football Club in the ardent hope that it makes their captain both proud and unworried by the esteem in which some of us hold him.

**HARTLEY SEBAG-FFIENNES,
ARSENAL SUPPORTER**

**A GOOD PASSING MOVE IS THE LIFE
BLOOD OF A MASTER SPIRIT**

When Arsenal prevail against their regional inferiors in the Temple of Football, it is a victory not just for the team but a victory for Civilisation – a victory not just for M. Wenger but for Keats, Baudelaire, Da Vinci, Woolf. Actually, "football" is too base and vulgar a word for what Arsenal, under the tutelage and guidance of M. Wenger, produce for the delectation of the better. This is not about feet and balls. Does one talk of Titian as a "brusher"? Herbert Von Karajan as a "Stick-waver"? Graham Greene as a "typist"? Which prompts one to pose the question. Why are Arsenal's fixtures written up in the sports pages and not the arts pages? Why was today's game broadcast on the coarse wavelength of "Radio 5 Live" and not Radio 3? Why have Arsenal yet to be featured on The South Bank Show? For these, and many other reasons, we have just reason to feel victimised. We should not be called "Arsenal" - we should be called

"Artenal".

(An explanatory note to any readers from outside North London: I created there what is known as a "pun". I replaced the letters "Ars" with the letters "Art". A further explanatory note: "Art" is the thing that hangs on walls, which you don't understand.)

To watch Arsenal's passing game is not merely to clutch one's head and scream "SOMEONE JUST BLOODY WELL SHOOT, FOR FUCKING FUCK'S SAKE! FUCK!!!!" It is to take an exquisite delight in pleasure constantly deferred; it is, in the angles, the sublime, reverberant and eternal joy of the hypotenuse. To watch the interplay between our plethora of graceful, bantamweight midfielders, toying with the opposition like Ariels against so many Calibans, is to be granted an audience with the very music of the spheres. It is to contemplate all that is elevated about the human condition, that which separates man from Mancunian.

One wonders if our base visitors from the North, from the regrettable municipality of Birmingham, for example, understand any of this. I must say in their defence that I have always felt that there is a wonderful quality of simplicity about the "Brummies". These bovine people, who find the multisyllabic nature of their very home town's name an insuperable barrier. As with farm animals, one could imagine, whimsically, what they might say if they could actually talk. As they were herded, thankfully downwind, into the away end, through an entrance with a sign reading "UNFORTUNATES", with a trough of water and some token straw laid on for them, jangling their little brown coins (question for The Guardian's "Notes And Queries" - are two pence pieces still in circulation in some parts of Britain?), I marvelled, as ever, that even to travel 150 miles outside of London is to travel aeons across the evolutionary scale. Show these people an aubergine, and they would doubtless lynch it on the spot, imagining it to be a diminutive asylum seeker. These regional troglodytes have yet to acquire the liberal, metropolitan qualities of broadmindedness and compassion.

What I find vexing is the absurd and misguided system whereby a team like Aston Villa, a team so agricultural that they could field a scarecrow as their centre back and no questions would be asked, are allowed to play a team like Arsenal, twice a season, when Arsenal's superiority is so self-evident and long established. It is as if the late poet laureate John Betjeman had been made to suffer the indignity, every few months, of having to pit his verses in competition against some faecal, Northern purveyor of lavatory wall doggerel, as if parity between the two were desirable, let alone imaginable. Of course, he did not. Why should Arsenal? They are, after all, by common consent, the Football Laureates. It would be better, I suggest, that until such time as M. Wenger shuffles off this mortal coil, these insulting fixtures between Arsenal and Aston Villa, or their fraternal counterparts Birmingham City, be suspended. They threaten to blight the escutcheon of the game. For, as we witnessed today, there is always the chance that, much as, monkey-like, a man from Birmingham or its outlying regions might, given enough time, write up the complete works of Shakespeare, so might a team from Birmingham, thanks to some bizarre concatenation of circumstances, somehow best Arsenal, at least in the minds of the Philistine bean counters who measure matches in terms of mere goals scored.

There are those, of course, who criticise Arsenal connoisseurs for making insufficient noise in support of their team, and for bringing altogether too many 19th-century French novels with them to games. To them, I say this. If one were to be transported back in time to the days of Jan Vermeer, as he sat at his easel painting The Lacemaker, would one contemplate sidling up and bellowing in his ear, "CCOMMONN, JAN! PAINT! PAINT! THATS IT! IN SPACE! PAINT IN THAT SPACE THERE!!! YESSS!!!" One would not. A sepulchral silence is the appropriate medium for a promising passing move from the back initiated by, par exemple, M. Clichy. (A further explanatory note to readers, particularly from Birmingham. The Lacemaker is a famous painting by Jan Vermeer, a Dutch artist. It hangs in The Louvre. The Louvre is an art gallery in Paris. Paris is the capital city of France. France is a country across the water, in mainland Europe. "Water" is a liquid substance with which people in London come into contact on a daily basis when they bathe, and not just occasionally when they fall into the canal while stumbling home inebriated.)

Small wonder it is, then, that, even as far away as Sheffield and Rotherham, Arsenal are as much envied as they are admired and loved. They are a beacon, a shining reminder of just how far the rest of you sub-people have to go, and how probable it is that you will fail in so doing. And so we cry, avanti! Senderos!

ENGLAND V MACEDONIA (European Championship qualifier) October 7, 2006

England drop their first points, thwarted in a disappointing home display with Gerrard picking up a yellow card that will rule him out of the Croatia fixture. The end of McClaren's winning streak – he is human after all, it seems.

EVER-SUPERLATIVE ENGLAND CRUSH, SUBJUGATE, OVERWHELM, SHOCK AND AWE MISERABLE MACEDONIANS 0-0

During the Second World War, as a senior interrogating officer attached to the British Intelligence Services, it fell to me to vet a number of partisans, supposedly under the aegis of Josef Tito, who had escaped the axis powers and were applying for shelter in the United Kingdom. A significant number of these partisans were from Macedonia, some of them women. As they sat opposite me, I must confess that, as a relatively young man in my early 40s, I did not always feel it easy to establish communications between myself and these swarthy, inscrutable females. I therefore made a point of requesting them to remove their scarves from about their faces before we commenced our interviews. Also, their shawls, blouses, girdles and brassieres. I was surprised that many of them obdurately refused to comply.

Such is the perversity, the refusal to accept certain realities, that pockmarks the national character of the Macedonians. Here, after all, is a nation whom England bested quite comprehensively in the paddock that passed for their own, home football ground, not a few days ago. Now, they presented themselves again, like a snivelling third-former at Rugby School, recently thrashed by the headmaster Dr Thomas Arnold, backside still crimson and throbbing, knocking at the door of Dr Arnold's study and requesting that the same treatment be meted out a second time. One's whiskers bristle at the sheer crust of these people.

And so, once again, England were compelled to line up and endure once more the Wagnerian tedium of the Macedonian national anthem, warbled punitively by some Irish chanteuse. Wayne Rooney shaved his beard for this match; by the end of the anthem, it had grown again. Thankfully, the rendition of our own anthem was delivered with such gusto that had Her Majesty deigned to open a window of Buckingham Palace she could have heard for herself John Terry's bellowing tones carried downwind from the province of Greater Manchester. The referee, Markus Merk, was a German. An ethnically sound choice, of course. However, one was paused to consider, had Mr Chamberlain not been so regrettably hotheaded in his handling of the Polish affair of 1939, might Mr Merk have been still more partial towards the English?

Of course, it was quite disgusting, and surely a matter for the leader writer of the Thunderer to ruminate upon, that given the surplus of Eastern Europeans currently flooding these shores, these 11 Macedonian men were allowed by immigration into this country at all. They may have claimed they had jobs to do; I contend that Englishmen could have performed the same jobs themselves - young apprentices, perhaps, donning red Macedonian shirts and offering token but futile resistance as England's brave boys notched up a hatful. What objection could UEFA have possibly have had to such an outcome? Political correctness, however, prevailed and the actual Macedonians were permitted to play the game, despite their patently subversive intentions. These, England sought to thwart at the outset, setting a high tempo. Some would regard England's first five minutes, during which they charged about at 95 miles per hour, as if rushing naked through the jungle with knives between their teeth, as an ill-advised waste of energy. The Macedonians, they would argue, stood and watched, then, as England ran out of energy, said, "OK, can we start now?" Nothing could be further from the truth. This was a demonstration to foreigners of all hues that although we English invented sanity in the 17th century, we are quite prepared to behave like complete madmen if it fazes our opponents.

In time, England fell into their more customary pattern of byzantine brilliance. Frank Lampard was Godlike and, like the Almighty, his active interventions gave no one any reason to doubt that He actually exists. Michael Carrick proved once again that, in acres of space, with time to consider his options, he is the undisputed master of the three-yard crossfield pass. Wayne Rooney scampered about like a puppy; it speaks volumes about the churlishness that poisons the Macedonian soul that they wouldn't let him have a touch of the ball. As for Stewart Downing, he must be the proudest lad in Britain. I had no idea that the light entertainment programme "Jim'll Fix It" was still being broadcast on the television channels. However, it was heartwarming to see that Mr Savile had evidently "fixed it" for young Master Downing to play alongside his grown-up heroes in a proper football game. Now, he can go back to his hometown of Middlesbrough, toepunting a can about with his young chums in the back alleyways, demonstrating how he nearly managed to kick the ball all the way from the touchline into the penalty area.

Supreme as ever, of course, was England's captain John Terry, especially in his passing. "When John Terry makes a pass at you, assume the appropriate position, as you can expect delivery of exquisite satisfaction from the rear." These words should be inscribed on the dressing room walls of every football stadium in the land, the better to be instilled in young footballing minds. His performance once again caused my exultation to approach a crest, and called for a warm hand.

In the second half, England created a host of chances, any one of which could have been taken. However, when presented with an open goal from two yards out, what was Gary Neville supposed to do? We had already beaten Macedonia; to have scored, under these circumstances, would have implied that there was somehow a doubt about our utter superiority, in all aspects but particularly the footballing, over these wretched Slavs. It would have besmirched our honour. Therefore, Mr Neville had no more choice than to blast over the bar. Peter Crouch faced the same dilemma with a free header just before the final whistle. He, too, remained admirably mindful of his duty as a patriot.

During the rare moments of tedium in this fixture, I jotted down certain thoughts. One was that every encouragement should be given to our transatlantic protégés the United States of America to expand their NASA project and invest billions, trillions, into space travel so that before the decade is out, we have discovered and made first contact with other planets, where atmospheric conditions have permitted the development of civilisations, so that England can travel across space to their countries and beat them at association football. Only then will we prevent absurd and insulting "double-ups", such as this unfortunate fixture. We need fresh nations to slaughter. It occurred to me too that, in order that to preclude the ghastly possibility that we be required to play Macedonia a third time in the future, this "independent" state should be re-merged into the Slav territories as a whole - by coercion, if they prove stubborn. A multi-nation task force, drawing from the English, Welsh, Irish and Scotch guards, could do the job, in a few weeks, goatherding up some of the other stray nations at bayonet-point while they are over there. The collective region could be known as "Balkanshire" and provisionally governed by some English person imbued with a sense of fair play and no nonsense; umpire Harold "Dickie" Bird springs to my mind. If one good thing has come from this match, then, it will be to restore peace, stability and common sense to a hitherto troubled part of the globe.

ENGLAND V CROATIA (European Championship qualifier)
October 11, 2006

England are beaten by a well-organised Croatia side, thanks to goals from the Brazilian-born Eduardo and an own goal from Gary Neville destined to live in infamy. Frank Lampard has an uncharacteristically anonymous game.

INCOMPARABLE, EFFORTLESS, SUPREME ENGLAND DESTROY COARSE, CONTEMPTIBLE CROATIA 0-2

At a recent fixture in Livorno against Italy, a group of Croatian supporters provoked wrath when they formed themselves into a human swastika. To witness such despicable appropriation of this symbol in the 21st century prompted the gorge to rise in all right-thinking people. What on earth did they think they were doing? Let us reflect upon what the swastika means. It is a symbol of racial superiority. Yet these supporters were Slavs!

How dare they presume parity with their Aryan betters? Slavs, I tell you, a mere "e" away from what many argue would be their true status if Civilisation in Europe were truly restored. A nation of petrol coupon traders, organ-grinders, goat-shearers, second-hand Skoda dealers, pomegranate juice drinkers, snipers, Jew's harpists and tractor-worriers who, having achieved independence in 1991 following a typically hotheaded collective outburst, found themselves in need of a national flag, and reached for the nearest tablecloth.

Such were the presumptuous curs ranged against England this night in this foreign dungpit they dared to call a stadium. Yet once again, our boys, our men, acquitted themselves superbly in a performance which included many positives, of which Gary Neville opening his account for his country was not even the most notable. What particularly caught the eye was that many of the England players, clad in gleaming white, departed the pitch with their kits as spotless as when they had lined up for the national anthems. This was the measure of our cleanly mettle. The savings in laundry bills will, furthermore, provide a much-needed boost to the national exchequer.

As the game commenced, the Croatians, vowel-less and soulless and with inhospitable insolence, appeared to be taking the upper hand. This was their home, Balkan territory; they knew every crevice, every undulation of that pitch, which of its lumps to cower behind and practise their sniper fire. England's men were not put out, however. There they stood, erect and lips curled, surveying the territory. Possession statistics and shots on target did not tell the story of who were the greater team; breeding and heritage are the true measures. This match was essentially won for England at Agincourt, and then again at Waterloo. Why it was being played a third time is a question for UEFA's blundering officials to answer.

Come the second half, and England began to express themselves. There's only one way to win a match like this and that's to charge, blast, thunder and scream until the opposition grow weary of picking the ball out from the gully in front of the advertising hoardings time and again, and eventually capitulate. It is a great pity that Steven Gerrard was not on the pitch tonight, giving vent to his talents. The same can be said of Frank Lampard. Michael Carrick displayed that even when churlishly harried by the opposition out of demonstrating his exhibition short passing skills, he is able to connect his foot with the ball as well as any man. Surely, after tonight, the matter of BBC television's Sports Personality Of The Year is settled. John Terry - well, one does not so much say things of John Terry as pant them, red-faced and repeatedly.

England had complete control of the game when, on the hour mark, a freakish event occurred. A Croatian launched a vague, aimless salvo deep into England territory, in breach of all international conventions - it was clear that our men were taking a much-needed tea break at the time. The ball hit the head of a Brazilian, who had mysteriously been smuggled onto the field of play, and floated into the net, despite Paul Robinson's perfect positioning. Point one: the goal should have been disallowed for offside. Granted, there were six English players between the Brazilian and the goal but, as replay footage shows, none of them were interfering with play in any way whatsoever. By my reading of the rules of the game, that renders the goal invalid. Even had it been counted, it should be awarded to the Brazilian Football Association, which should come as a pleasant surprise to that ramshackle footballing body. In any case, until FIFA respond to my letter on the subject, the issue of the "goal" remains suspended.

Minutes later came a further shock. Gary Neville delivered a routine backpass to goalkeeper and doughty John Bull Yorkshireman Paul Robinson. The ball took a bobble and trundled calamitously into that sanctum of sanctums, the English net. There was laughter in the cells of The Hague as the moment sank in. And, to the non-observant, it might have seemed like Robinson could not have looked a greater fool had he been wearing a huge yellow wig and been driven around the penalty area in a backfiring car with a dog in a fireman's helmet at the wheel. However, closer scrutiny reveals that he was clearly the hero of the hour. As the ball approached, Robinson was aware that the lump that lay before him was most probably a dormant incendiary device of some sort. Had he struck the ball, he risked setting off the device, thus triggering an explosion and subsequent firestorm which would have brought the entire stadium burning down in minutes, resulting in the deaths of dozens, maybe hundreds of English people. And so, at the very last minute, like a Spitfire pilot taking evasive action, he swerved his foot into harmless mid-air, thereby saving lives. That he then jumped about on the device, in the manner of the animated cartoon character popular in the United States Of America, Mr Wile E Coyote, is not inconsistent with this theory: it merely demonstrates that Yorkshiremen like Robinson, though brave as they come, are not as generously endowed with intelligence.

As the final whistle beckoned, England surged forward in numbers, winning corner after corner, the Croatians utterly demoralised and yearning, if not for their post-match bath (this was Eastern Europe), then to be worked over by an old woman with a mop. If this had been a boxing match, it would have been called off by the referee, as England had their quarry on the ropes and were pounding away. Indeed, the match should have been called off and John Terry's hand held aloft. The referee, however, was an Italian. Such a decision would have taken courage and, as we all know, the closest equivalent to the word "courage" in the Italian language is "couraga", which turns out to be a regional speciality, a pesto derived from crab juice.

To suggest any amendment in England's formation is to gild the lily. However, although 3-5-2 served us well, for our next game, I would suggest the following;

IN GOAL: Robinson, James, Shilton, Banks.

DEFENCE: Cole, Neville, Neville, Neville, Ferdinand, Woodgate, Campbell, Stiles

MIDFIELD: Cole, Cole, Cole, Hargreaves, Carrick, Carragher, Gerrard, Lampard, Charlton (J)

ATTACK: Defoe, Bent, Walcott, Rooney, Crouch, Heskey, Johnson, Shearer, Charlton (R)

4-8-9-9. Overwhelming superiority in numbers - the secret to any successful campaign.

One further addendum for dispatches: that following his selfless heroics on the pitch, Paul Robinson be recommended for the Victoria Cross, at a ceremony to be arranged at the earliest convenience at the Palace. While there, the growing lobby for a knighthood for Steve McClaren, which is fast taking on the dangerous dimensions of mob dissatisfaction, could be sated also. Dub him "Sir Steve" with all available dispatch, ma'am, if you value your railings!

ENGLAND V HOLLAND (Friendly)
November 15, 2006

England seem on course to salvage some pride following the Croatia defeat, with a Rooney goal, his first at international level for over year, in a drab fixture in Amsterdam. However, Holland pull level late on thanks to another uncharacteristic defensive error.

HONEST, DOUGHTY ENGLAND SHOW DUTCH WHAT COURAGE IS TRULY MADE OF IN 1-1 ROUT

Ah, England, my England. Literally my England, in the case of several thousand acres of it, as numerous backpacking trespassers have had cause to reflect upon as they pick buckshot out of the seat of their corduroys. What has England bequeathed to the world? The Bard of Avon. The four-minute mile. The sandwich. Gravity. Football, both codes. Penicillin. Electricity. Common sense. Field Marshall Montgomery. Fair play. Benevolent colonial rule. The Penny Farthing. The lavatory. Rudyard Kipling. High tea. The fagging system. The grimy chimney sweep. The finest navy on the high seas. Her Royal Highness the late Princess Margaret. The oratory of Winston Churchill. "Land of Hope and Glory". The steam engine. The industrial revolution. What, by contrast, have our foes upon the footballing field this night, the Dutch, given us? Elm disease.

And so it was that England's mighty oaks were ranged against a nation of slimy and perfidious tree killers, clad in clownish orange. The national anthems were, as ever, so effective an indicator of the better 11 that had the referee not been a Slovenian, he would have called off the game there and then. But then, what is to be expected of a man who doubtless arrived in Western Europe by dint of clinging to the undercarriage of a lorry? England hailed our Queen with a lusty yodel. However, when the Dutch delivered their own anthem, doubtless based around the theme of bicycles, they did so with such unseemly volume that it was impossible to hear the booing of the English fans. This was unwarrantable. In England, we have such as thing as a democracy. Every man has his say without let or hindrance. Evidently, in Holland, it is the policy for the voice of the sensible minority to be drowned out.

The match commenced, with no immediate incident. Then, following a delay, John Terry took the opportunity to gather his team for a pep talk. He went round to each man in turn and, following a kind word to each, shook them firmly and briskly by the penis - the team having elected to divest of their kit at this point and face the enemy as God had intended. Then, the captain appeared to spot me in the stands, and floated towards me, striding manfully across the clouds of glory in which he is customarily wreathed . . . we were about to embrace as men, when my Great Aunt Gertrude appeared, waggling an admonishing finger. "Hateful, filthy little boy!" But Auntie . . .

It was at this point I was aware of my manservant Seppings shaking me gently. Evidently, I had dozed off, for the clock indicated that 30 minutes had passed. How I had managed to sleep through the cannon's roar of England's mighty onslaught upon the Dutch goal I shall never fathom. Still, I continued to watch in fascination as Michael Carrick delivered an exquisite, arcing, perfectly weighted 50-yard crossfield ball into touch, causing panic in the Dutch ranks, unconvincingly masked by expressions of unworried amusement.

England, naturally, caught the eye and stole the breath with their commitment, alertness, aplomb and vigour. Young Micah Richards particularly scampered about with great enthusiasm, eager to please. He reminded me of a boy I kept back in my days in the colonies, a very able and attentive fellow, though I was obliged to have him tied to a tree for some minor infraction involving a fish fork. The screams ceased after three days; the lions got to him, I daresay. The Dutch defences were lamentable, but this was of no surprise to military historians. The Netherlands' Home Guard might as well have consisted of several ranks of tulips during World War II. The Dutch can no more defend than they can talk properly. After all, what is their so called "language" if not the woeful attempts of a backward people to speak English, hampered by their tongues having swollen through unwisely licking the bark of an elm tree? "Vaart" "Vrooood" "Kupyt". This isn't talking, man, it's yelping. Though clear through with the Dutch team having fled to their attics rather than challenge them, both Gerrard and Rooney deliberately chose not to score but to tap the ball into the goalkeeper's hands, mindful that the humiliation of letting the Dutch off in such a manner would be worth far more than a mere goal in the final tally of things.

England eventually could not help scoring and could have run out 20- or 30-nil victors, forming a conga line to tap the ball in every 30 seconds or so. That they chose not to is a testimony to their restraint and a courtesy to their hosts, though doubtless all it would take to claim Holland for the Empire would be the dispatch across the North Sea of two battalions of Sea Scouts armed with catapults. England toyed with the Dutch in the second half; then, however, with unspeakable rudeness (or "ruuuuudnyssss", as they would doubtless have it), the Dutch pulled a goal back from a throw-in, in a particularly shabby and low piece of play from the low countrymen. When going for the ball, England's defence rose as one, in the "All for one and one for all" spirit that has seen us through many a dark hour. It's in our blood. Whereupon a sneaky Dutch fellow took advantage of this spontaneous show of national unity to caper into the large opening it left and punt the ball miserably home. The game's ending in a draw had the effect of very slightly tarnishing what was an excellent victory for England.

Two things emerge from this triumph. The first concerns criticisms from Hansen, the Scotchman hired by the British Broadcasting Corporation, that Andrew Johnson was being played too far out to the right, as if a drift to the far right were somehow a bad thing. After all, had England not sensibly drifted to the far right in the late 1970s, we would all today be speaking Argentinean, and/or obliged to carry about a small notebook containing the thoughts of Denis Healey. Johnson's performance alone indicated that manager Steve McClaren most certainly has the faintest, remotest bloody clue what he is doing.

The second is that, with our European Championship rivals Croatia and Russia playing on the same day and earning points, it is preposterous that the points England accrued in this fixture are discounted from inclusion in the qualifying table, thanks to some quibbling, bureaucratic insistence on UEFA's part. It appears that in this day and age it is one rule for the English and another for the foreigners. What folly it was to join the Common Market when we are subject to this sort of madness. To play a "friendly", it seems, is to be docked points. Very well. We shall play hostile. Attention all sea scouts!

ENGLAND V SPAIN (Friendly)
February 7, 2007

England's first home defeat, thanks to a goal from Iniesta, following an uncharacteristically poor defensive clearance from Rio Ferdinand. John Terry replaced by the headbanded, injury prone Jonathan Woodgate. Doubts about Gerrard and Lampard's ability to gel in midfield.

BRILLIANT BRITONS SCUPPER AND REPEL SPANISH SUB-MONKEY ARMADA 0-1

This fixture was hampered by controversy before a ball had been kicked in anger. For at the two teams' previous meeting, fans of the Spanish team had chanted in a Simian-like manner throughout much of the game. Reporters at the time erroneously ascribed these outbursts to some sort of racialism directed at England's negro players. Alas, they lacked the benefit of my own insight into the Spanish, having witnessed them at first hand. These were not noises of derision on the part of these creatures, but rather of wistful aspiration. I laid all this clear in the 1930s in a short volume, published at my own expense, entitled "Did Apes Evolve From Spaniards?" The evidence, to wit, the presence of a breakaway colony of the Barbary variety in nearby Gibraltar, is pretty clear; they did. The Gibraltarians have become monkeys, with time; the Spanish have yet to do so. Hence, when I travelled to the country during the Civil War in the 1930s with my then-batman Seppings, I distinguished myself in that I was the only participant in the hostilities to be fighting against both sides, Republicans and Nationalists alike. I saw no ideological difference, only Spaniards, and shot every last donkey-abusing, flea-ridden, influenza-bearing bally jack of them I set eyes on.

It was against this backdrop of Darwinian envy and still-simmering hostility that this fixture took place. It was perhaps the most significant in which England have taken part in years. For at stake here was the very principle of evolutionary superiority. You could divine its importance in the gleam of the England players' eyes as they lined up for the national anthem, and in the awestruck way in which the jaw of Rio Ferdinand, the finest Englishman since Bernard Bresslaw, hung open, moving in time to the verses. As for the Spanish team, one felt almost a pang of sympathy for them: for their zookeeper had clearly, out of mischief, arranged for some coiffeur to work on them beforehand, decking them out in a variety of amusingly preposterous haircuts, as compromising to their animal dignity as is a tutu to a performing bear.

There were numerous changes to the English line-up, with one Ben Foster replacing Paul Robinson as goalkeeper. This was of no consequence since English goalkeeper, like Lord Mayor of London, is essentially a ceremonial position – there is generally very little for him to do. Kieron Dyer also joined the England ranks and acquitted himself superbly. It would be grossly inappropriate had he been born with the Christian names "Absolutely Bloody", such was his performance. It is similarly proper that England's right winger should be called "Wright-Phillips" and not "Wright-Twat", so effective was he. Full, marks, also, to manager Steve McClaren, for courageously selecting young Phil Neville at left back – a rare chance indeed to see what kind of place he might have in England's future.

The game began at a cracking pelt, with Peter Crouch proving, as ever, that he functions as more than an early warning system in case it should start to snow. The Spaniards panicked and clattered into each other divertingly, all but running back to the safety of the cages in which they arrived at Old Trafford. The remainder of the first half was full of twists, turns and pleasant surprises from the English team, such as discovering, after some 40 minutes, that Frank Lampard was on the pitch. However, the game as a whole will be remembered as a masterclass in the art of the short pass from Maestro Michael Carrick. It was like watching some elaborate waltz from better days. Carrick delivers two-yard pass to Gerrard; returns to his stationary position in front of the back four; looks quietly pleased with himself. Carrick delivers one-yard pass to Kieron Dyer; Dyer falls over; Carrick reassumes stationary position and air of modesty. Carrick attempts 40-yard pass, which successfully confounds the Spanish, who were expecting the ball to stay on the field rather than high up in the cheap seats.

The second half saw England dominate once more and was not without incident. A Spaniard fell injured at one point, all but requiring the attention of the veterinarian who travels with their team. A free kick was awarded to England when the refereeing official might have done better to play "advantage"; then again, this is a moot point since, being English, they are always at an advantage. It was a touching gesture on England's part, I felt, to allow the Spanish a consolation goal midway through the second half; after all, they have a long journey back home, in their crates. As the full time whistle blew, the English fans made their feelings for the Spaniards clear with a loud chorus of boos; no doubt, later, there would be a cry of "Three cheers for Steve McClaren! Hip! Hip! Hooray" and the unanimous tossing of caps in the air, but by that point, the broadcast had finished. I must say, the British Broadcasting Corporation did not distinguish themselves on this night; due, doubtless, to a blunder on the part of one of their typists, the result was mistakenly flagged up as England 0, Spain 1. So mesmerising was the action that I admit I fell into a trance for long periods of the game and so missed England's hatful of goals. I shall, however, be dictating to Seppings a letter for the immediate attention of the Director General, scolding him for this crass error and calling for the person responsible if not to be sacked, then certainly horsewhipped.

If I entertain any small doubt about England's performance tonight, it is this: that the playing of sporting matches between the species should perhaps not be encouraged, in case, by some admittedly unimaginable accident, the inferior species prevails and begins to develop ideas beyond its evolutionary station. Granted, there is a history of such fixtures – one thinks of the American negro athlete who regularly raced against horses – however, I would advise the Football Association to be more circumspect in future.

Furthermore, despite his injury it was, perhaps, a mistake for England's captain, hero and just the man you need when you want to come from behind, John Terry, not to have been selected. In his stead played a fellow with a headband apparently concealing some sort of lobotomy scar. If not Terry in person, then Terry in effigy should be planted, scarecrow-like on the edge of the English penalty box, terrifying the oncoming foe. I have one in my own garden, which the Football Association could rent at friendly rates. It would serve as a model of typical English defensive obduracy and mobility.

INAPPROPRIATE CHAMPIONSHIP MANAGER

Reflecting on a recent string of disappointing results in the lower division

Vs CARDIFF, 0-3 (a)

It's never easy. Cardiff are never easy to play. We know that. Everyone knows that. So, nobody's expecting miracles. On the other hand, we are expected to maintain a certain threshold. For instance, it's one thing for a feller to make love to his father-in-law. But to make love to his father-in-law when he's been dead for two hours, that's quite another thing. That's crossing a line. And we crossed that line today, make no mistake.

Vs COVENTRY, 0-4 (h)

It wasn't the result we were looking for, no. And it's easy for heads to drop at a time like this. But it's a bit like dog crucifixion. There are always going to be the naysayers trying to mess with your mind. You've got the RSPCA lot saying it's cruel, you've got the Christians saying it's sacrilegious or whatever, and you know, you can't please everybody. But what you do is, you block out those negative voices, you pull the dog back by the ears, take the hammer out from between your teeth and nail its paws to the door, job done. And then the whining stops but until then, by Heaven! That's football. All it takes is a bit of belief in yourself and for people to believe in you in turn and what you're trying to do with this dog, this club.

Vs WEST BROMWICH ALBION, 0-3

Yes, I'll hold my hands up and say, it's not the curtain raiser to the new season we were looking for. We, this football club, we were looking to lay down a marker but if you go one down against a team like West Brom and don't adapt to their attacking formation, you will be punished. This team mustn't be afraid to experiment. It's like, you know, we know, the stresses and strains of this job. So, you're away one night, taking your pleasure with a particular seasoned lady of a certain age whose services you've used in the past, you and the Wayne Rooneys of this world, shall we say. And you've been going at it some time when suddenly she seizes up, turns a shade of blue and, well, to be fair, dies. On the job, like Tommy Cooper, the way she would have wanted. So, you think, well, you've paid your money, so you keep banging away, and then it occurs to you – here's a chance to experiment. So, with all due respect, you turn her over onto her front and, well, there you go. That's what this team has to do. Whether it's a tricky opposition or a dead prostitute, you have to be prepared to do something a little bit different.

Vs READING, 0-6 (h)

Are the owners of this club losing patience? Well, at the end of the day you'd have to ask them that question. So far as I'm concerned, I've an excellent relationship with them, I know where I stand. It's like buying dwarves off the internet. Oh yes, you can, there's a website, they're Eastern European, mainly. You break open the crate, the little feller's a bit dazed at first, but you show him the pen you've set up for him in the back garden, you fatten him up with a few tins of Alphabetti Spaghetti, teach him some circus tricks and after six weeks, you've got a barbecue set up in the back garden for friends and you're firing him out of a miniature cannon onto a trampoline, you know, as enter-tainment. That's football. We're here to entertain but it's the owners' club to do as they please with, the same as it's my dwarf to do as I please with – until he gets chewed to pieces by the family Alsatian, that is. That's the real world.

ENGLAND V ISRAEL (European Championship qualifier)
March 24, 2007

A dismal stalemate, which brings the first serious cries of discontent from the England crowd. Andrew Johnson again fails to shine, except in the gleam of his pate.

EXCELLENT ENGLAND SHOW BOTH AERIAL AND ARYAN SUPERIORITY AS ISRAEL DENIED POUND OF FLESH IN 0-0 THRILLER

Of course, what strikes any observer is that, this being the European Championships, it is quite absurd that one of the countries participating is not actually European at all. I speak of England, of course. We are not "Europeans", whatever some preposterous, brilliantine, pinstripe little Belgian jobsworth with a briefcase full of regulations might insist. We are English, our sovereign's profile gracing our currency, our spirits unbroken, our bananas unbent. It is the natural advantage we bring into every association football game. And what made us, happy breed that we are? The hardening experiences of the Second World War, that is what. Let me tell you one story. It concerns myself. During the aforementioned hostilities, I was detained for several months at the Chancellor's pleasure in the prison of war camp Colditz. One afternoon, while in the exercise yard, I was confronted by a young German Lieutenant, bristling with a presumptuous air that at once got my gander up. "Herr Captain!" he barked. "A word with you, sir, if you please." Whereupon I reddened visibly, strode over and with two deft flicks, set about the impertinent little sausage grinder with my riding crop. How dare he? I was not a Captain, I was a Major-General, dash it all. I was summoned before the Camp Commandant. My punishment was severe indeed: confined to barracks for a week; my brandy rations suspended for five days; my riding crop temporarily confiscated. However, I endured it, dreadful as the privation was, with character. No Jew could possibly understand what we English went through in the Second World War: such adversity, deprivations, such hardships. However, the improving effects these experiences would have on our island racial stock were the difference between the two teams tonight.

We were up against it in this fixture, that is for sure. We had just the plain, stout yeomen of our embattled, sceptr'd isle from which to pick our team, whereas our opponents had the teeming mass of international Jewry at their grasping disposal. However, a nation whose best citizens can go days without brandy, like some camel of the desert, are sufficient in fortitude to cope with such blatant disadvantage.

The national anthems were, as ever, part endurance, part unbridled joy. The Israelite anthem was a dirge. Good God, people, what's with the long faces? Pull your socks up and buck up those ideas while you're at it! Not like our own, merry national anthem, which is impossible to listen to without getting up and dancing (while simultaneously saluting, naturally). But then, the Hebrews are a strange people. I am closely acquainted with their sort. I made a large fortune some decades ago running a successful string of kibbutzim; the look on the faces of those youngsters, believing, mistakenly as it happened, that their 12 hours a day of back-breaking labour had all been for some collective, communitarian effort was touching indeed. However, years later, when a string of investments in Bolivian old people's homes went awry, I fell onto hard times and was forced to take up a position as coach and mentor at a training camp for young Jewish footballers in the Golders Green district. I remember what turned out to be my final address to the camp team, in the presence of their parents and other camp officials, just minutes before my dismissal. I recall it as if it were yesterday. It was on the eve of a vital fixture.

"Now see here, camp!" I boomed. "Tomorrow's match is of the utmost importance. Second place in the regional division is at stake. The points we garner will be vital. In order to procure them, camp, you must at all times maintain focus. Do not let your attention waver, camp. Fix solely upon the matter in hand, which is to win every ball, to successfully contest every challenge. Only by these means will you prevail. Remember, concentration, camp, is the final solution."

What happened next was quite astonishing. There was an audible, collective gasp and I was bundled off the premises by two burly fellows. I cannot imagine what I said to cause such offence; it was suggested that I made inadvertent illusion to some mistreatment the Jews were alleged to have suffered at the hands of the Germans during World War II; these rumours were later summarily scotched, however, by a British historian so I cannot see what the fuss was about. It seems that if we must draw one lesson from the 20th century it is this: never underestimate the excessive sensitivity of the Hebrew.

It was England's intention to impose themselves on the Israelites from the very moment of the kick off, and this they did - it was to their credit that such was their relentless attacking force and retention of possession that Israel made fewer than nine attacks upon the England goal in the first ten minutes alone. Arik Banado, a Jew, passed to Amit Ben Shushan, another Jew, as they tried to advance. However, Rio Ferdinand and co merely stood off and laughed, forming a defensive wall against which the Israelites could only wail in frustration.

Upfront, it was not a case of if, but when England would score, how frequently, and whether the Israeli nets would have to be replaced before half time as goal after goal rained in. England had complete control. Aaron Lennon made several surging runs down the flank, sometimes with the ball actually at his feet. Frank Lampard and Steven Gerrard solved the conundrum of whether they can play together in the same team brilliantly, by the expedient of neither of them playing at all in the first 20 minutes. With the "big one" against Andorra in mind, Wayne Rooney wisely preserved his energies. Jamie Carragher, every time he exhorted them to push forward, drenched his teammates in a cooling, refreshing shower of phlegm to counter the Tel Aviv heat. Tribute must be paid to Steve McClaren, however, in both halves, for he has succeeded in imprinting his character on the English style of play. They played tonight, it must be said, with an undeniable "McClaren-ness". It was if the very rhythms of their play seemed to whisper, then shout "McClaren! McClaren! McClaren!" like some old locomotive engine gathering momentum, with the steam whistle emitting the occasional, high-pitched "Steeeeeve! Steeevve!" in moments of high excitement. Not for England the fleet-footed, unexpected style of some of their more hotheaded opponents. England's play and build-up was slow and predictable for an excellent reason: in order to demonstrate, slowly and patiently, to foreigners how the game should be played, as if showing an imbecilic Mediterranean waiter the correct method of brewing a cup of tea.

The English crowd certainly appreciated the manager's methods as the curtain came down on another superb and scintillating English performance. They bade him emerge from his dugout to take their plaudits with moving cries of "McClaren out! McClaren out!" Yes, out you come, Mr McClaren, take a bow.

This was more than a mere association football match. Other values were at stake, and among them was the value of a good foreskin. No one represents these values better than England's captain and inspiration, John Terry. How I wish the Football Association had acceded to my written request that John Terry's foreskin be painted in the white and red striped colours of the Flag of St. George before the match, as a symbol of our pride in this matter. I am not suggesting that he take to the field sans shorts in order to display the daubed markings; Her Majesty would doubtless be tuning in to watch the game and the protection of her unbruised sensibilities must be of paramount concern. However, in close midfield clashes with the opposition, he could have discreetly opened his shorts to offer a brief glimpse of the foreskin to the Israelis, the better to sap their spirit.

I'd further aver that England's triumph tonight should be the spur for England, the nation, to take advantage of our political leverage in the region and to implement a solution to what might be called the Hebrew Question, which seems to have arisen despite the excellent efforts of British civil servants back in the 1940s. It seems that there is some competition between the Jews and the Arabs for territory, in the "Promised Land". Well, since both sides have shown themselves unable to behave like gentlemen, I propose that both peoples be displaced and the land be put at the disposal of English property developers to build much-needed homes, both for the retired and young English couples looking to "start up" and breed English children. The new territory could be named "Anglestine". Some of the Arab peoples could stay on in menial roles, such as functioning as mobile, human hand-driers for those English people who suffer from perspiring palms in the hot climate of the Middle East. The Jews could wander off somewhere else, which, as the Good Book tells us, is their historical wont in any case. As if there were not enough positive outcomes from this match, this would be yet another.

ENGLAND V ANDORRA (European Championship qualifier)
March 28, 2007

England are jeered off after failing to score in the first 45 minutes in a fixture held at Barcelona's Nou Camp. Steven Gerrard finally spares McClaren's blushes. Substitute David Nugent scores from extremely close range. Wayne Rooney again manages to mislay his temper and will miss the Estonia match.

ASTONISHING ENGLAND PREVAIL 3-0 IN THE NOU CAMP CAULDRON

"Grand Vizier of the Andorran Principality! Assorted goatherders! A lonely sheep, bleating on an Andorran mountaintop! Arnau, the slow-witted customs official! Lothario, the local pervert! Your frustrated, seven-year-old centre forward! Jose, the Andorran mascot! A goat! Another goat! And another one! Your boys took a hell of a beating!"

Such was the cry that surely rang out from every English

commentary box as England pulled off perhaps one of the greatest results of their proud history, and one which will surely guarantee not merely a knighthood for the recent honoured Steven Gerrard MBE but his imminent beatification – unless, perhaps, His Holiness the Pope fancies the chances of the Vatican City football team against our mighty heroes! After tonight, I think not. For even Papal infallibility would be jeopardised by the superhuman efforts of Cole, Dyer, and, lest we forget, Wayne "The Effective" Rooney and Stewart "The Non-Useless, Useless, Useless, Do You Hear Me, Absolutely Hopelessly And Cluelessly Useless" Downing.

For years to come, commentators will speak in awestruck, breathless tones of "That night in Barcelona" - for that night was this night. However, do not labour under any misapprehension: this, our finest hour, was preceded by our darkest. The weasels of the benighted Fourth Estate had dared to suggest, despite England's recent string of superlative results, that all was not well within the England set-up, and that (deplore their perfidy) an Italian should perhaps take over the reins of management – a suggestion akin to the News Chronicle, in 1940, proposing that Mr Rudolf Hess take over as Prime Minister in place of Neville Chamberlain. As the playwright Christopher Marlowe once wrote, "let their heads preach upon poles, for trespass of their tongues"! But we shall deal with them later.

They say it only takes a second to score a goal and, by that calculation, England could have won 5,400-0 over the 90 minutes. That would have been an acceptable result. But this was not that sort of game. This was an away match and the crowd duly expressed their hostility, booing England at every oppor-tunity in the first half. Moreover, our own Wayne Rooney was subject to a constant stream of insinuations from the bearded cur appointed to mark him. One can only guess what he was whispering, in close conference, in Rooney's ears: "You're a potato-shaped waste of space. What talent you've got you've spunked away, like you did your load in that geriatric prostitute. When you're 27, you'll be as wide as you are tall and eking out a living doing karaoke versions of Grumbleweeds songs. Your wife is a parasitic slapper who will suck you dry and spit out your blubbery husk when you're done with, which is sooner than you think: we're talking months, not years. When your legs go and you can't get a game in Burnley reserves, you'll be regretting you didn't take the opportunity to learn to talk when you were at school, you walnut-brained, rancid lump of drain-blocking lard. You'll be pissing in a prison bucket before you hit 30, and probably missing the bucket most of the time, judging by your recent games. You've got two nostrils: use them, you missing fucking link." Thankfully, Rooney ignored these baseless taunts with the pacifistic forbearance of a Bertrand Russell.

With the odds stacked against them, England were nonetheless superlative in the first half. Ashley Cole translated the impact he's made on the literary scene onto the pitch. Andy Johnson showed that he was not overawed by the opposition – these may have been postmen, stationmasters and supply teachers he was playing against but in his eyes, they were just human beings, players with two legs just like him and he responded accordingly, entering the Andorran penalty box more than once with intent. As for Frank Lampard, he was as effective in this game as he has been in his last several appearances.

In the second half, Steven Gerrard stepped up to the plate. As all of England watched, in hamlets, youth clubs, church associations, freemasons' lodges, public houses, wherever a television was to be found, the fear was that the Andorrans, on home turf, would inevitably prevail against our plucky boys. And yet, astonishingly, against all odds, it was Gerrard, yes, Steven Gerrard, who opened the scoring! The nation whooped as one in gratitude and utter astonishment. Could England conceivably snatch not just the draw we all hoped for but the victory we dared not dream of, in the fortress that is the Nou Camp? Surely not. The

Andorrans pressed on, with the wrath of a wounded Goliath, and yet, back came England and, with yet another slingshot from the blue, the young David Gerrard smote the foe with a second! By this point, the church bells were ringing across the Empire, the youth of England were doing congas around England's village maypoles and there was dancing in the fountains of Trafalgar Square. The pandemonium was redoubled when young Nugent added a third, yes, a third, and into the bargain showed that there is no more deadly a striker from one inch out than he.

Two things emerge from this fixture. The first is that, in response to Andorra invading the England half not once but twice in the duration of these 90 minutes, our forces should be mobilised and, in vengeance for this provocative act of impudence, we dispatch a task force of several aircraft carriers, Trident-bearing submarines, several squadrons of the RAF's finest, SAS shock troops and 30,000 troops made up of regulars and Territorial Army backup to claim Andorra as our own. If we show the spirit, character, character, spirit, guts, character and guts, not to say spirit, that Mr McClaren praised in our boys upon the football field tonight, I'd give our forces a fighting chance of seeing off the Andorrans.

The second is that reports in the newspaper of record, delivered daily to me by Seppings, my manservant, once ironed, suggest that there were those who doubted England's capacity to pull off the famous victory they achieved tonight. These naysayers are quislings and should be treated with the same contempt as did our neighbours the French their own collaborators. They deserve to be birched in the town squares and I can think of no better a man than our captain and inspiration, John Terry, to administer that birching. He could make a tour of the cities and market towns, his ever-ready cane twitching like a traitor-diviner, his nostrils flaring with patriotic scorn. In fact, mea culpa – I myself temporarily doubted that England would prevail during the first half. For this, Mr Terry, I too deserve the full wrath of your birch. Do not spare me, nor stint in your strokes.

Two years on from That Night In Istanbul, Liverpool meet AC Milan again – in Athens. This time, Liverpool go down 2-1. SELF RIGHTEOUS LIVERPOOL SUPPORTER reflects on the game, marred by ticketing irregularities and a claim by a UEFA spokesman, later denied, that Liverpool had the "worst fans in Europe".

IT'S NOT WHAT LIVERPOOL DO, IT'S WHAT WE ARE – THE TRAGEDY OF ISTANBUL
May 24, 2007

In this time of total national grief I take comfort in the Alternative Book Of Scouse Jokes. That's all the usual ones, right, but with alternative endings written by a true Scouser who understands Scouse, ie me, so it's The Truth.

Q: What do you call a Liverpudlian in a suit?

A: Degsy Hatton. A man who stood proud and walked tall for the people of Liverpool, only to be betrayed by Southerners who were prejudiced against all Liverpudlians just because of the way they talk and the colour of their skin. But he will return and so will we, hope in our hearts.

Q: Why do all Liverpudlians wear shellsuits?

A: They don't. They don't, right. I mean, some do. I do and all my mates do. But some don't, I suppose. Not always. Because we're all different. And Scousers are more different from anybody than anybody. You'd understand if you were a Scouser. But you're not. We are.

See, that's real humour that. From a true comedian, ie me. That's why people laugh at me. Laugh their bollocks off every time I open my mouth. Because we're all comedians up here, eh? One on every street corner, in every doorway, in every bus shelter. All forged from the same adversity and passion and sense of community that forges a Tom O'Connor. But tonight wasn't about laughter. Tonight was about the pride, the passion, the glory and the pride. Who could believe it, eh? 2005. Liverpool meet Milan in the Champions League final in Istanbul. Two years later, same two teams, same final. And the same city. It's called DESTINY. Spell it out, D-E-C-C-C-C-C-C-C-H-H-H-H-H-H-S-S-S-S-S-T-I-N-Y. For one long year the European Cup has been missing from its true home. This is a national tragedy. As the banner I made to take on my long trek to the final read: Pray For Maddie. Pray For Liverpool.

Of course, it costs money, like, to get to a place like Istanbul. But y'know, there's always a way. A bit of jibbing, ducking and diving. But it's also about working together. Like me and my mates. We raised the money by burgling each other's houses. Left our doors open for one another. That's community. That's cooperation. That's passion. That's heart. You don't get that in a city like Everton.

Anyway, it's the big day and here we were in Istanbul. Looked in at the bar and you could see on the telly Liverpool supporters all gathered as far away as Athens, chanting the chant, never walking alone. That's how it is on nights like this. Liverpool IS Europe. But when we got to Istanbul stadium we hardly noticed any fellow reds. So the media stories of UEFA quite literally withdrawing tickets from ALL true Liverpool fans because they hate our passion and our pride were dead true. We get to the stadium, we're the only ones there. No tickets but loads of Scouse charm. "Lerrus in, mate", I says to the moustached feller on the door. "Lerrus in, like. I've left me ticket back at the hotel but I'll go fetch it and show you it after the game, like, honest." Actually that was just a bit of brilliant Scouse cunning but still I was dead offended when this woolyback looks at me like he half doesn't believe me! Tarring us all with the same brush, like.

"You want to see reserve game here, you need ticket," he says. Come 'ed? Anyway, we tried to force the door open for 25 minutes till finally it dawned on us - those UEFA bastards had switched the venue at the last minute. We burst into tears - we must have been teargassed by the Turks - and go and watch in the bar. Come on, Liverpool! Stevie, Jamie! Stevie! The game started and Stevie Gerrard, I tell you, what a man. What a man. Every time he got the ball he was blasting it high and wide, deliberately aiming it into the stands. He knew how much them balls would be worth to a Liverpool fan on e-Bay the next day, to sell on, to put food on their tables, hope in their hearts and Kestrel lager in their bellies. Putting the fans first, that's Stevie. For my money that alone gave us a moral one goal lead, to add to the one Liverpool fans are worth every game which should have had us 2-0 up but then Inter Milan got one and Jamie Carragher tackled and tackled, the way he does all night for fun and then Inter Madrid got another and Stevie Gerrard gave us hope and pride and we got one back. But then the ref got scared and blew the whistle and once again, just like in the Eighties, Liverpool were the victims of a footballing tragedy that will touch the hearts and minds of all peoples, Liverpudlians and Evertonians alike, but from which Liverpool will emerge taller, strengthened as a community, reborn in a valley of tears, Christlike and Godlike.

But now was the time to think of suing some bastard. Get on the phone to one of them daytime telly lawyer firms and sue. Sue UEFA for moving the fixture to Athens, not Istanbul like last time. Sue Inter Milan for deliberately sabotaging our offside trap with their cynical tactics. You don't do that to a man like Jamie Carragher. Sue Rafa Benitez for not putting on Robbie Fowler, at least for the last 89 minutes. Sue that Clive Tyldesley for deliberately building up our hopes - some of us put our life savings on at Paddy Power at half time on account of the way he was going on. It's not right. Sue The Beatles for abandoning Liverpool in its hour of need. Sue Man Utd for not tiring Milan out enough in the semi final. Sue the Government for the whole Degsy Hatton scandal. Sue Starbucks for taking a significant part of their name from Liverpool's finest golfer and comedian, Jimmy T himself, the man known to one and all quite simply as "The Joke".

But this is no joke. Come the first weekend of the new season, there should be a minute's silence at every football ground in the United Kingdom for Liverpool's lost trophy. Who knows where it is now? In foreign hands, I dunno, Spain, Italy, wherever Inter Madrid or Milan is, asking over and over when it can come home to Anfield and get to see it's true Da' again, Stevie Gerrard. It's heartbreaking. But no one loses like Liverpool. We will return to Istanbul, for another That Night. We will be back. And this time, we'll lose by more.

ENGLAND V BRAZIL (Friendly)
June 1, 2007

The first international at the new Wembley Stadium is crowned by a headed goal from John Terry, before Diego equalises with a headed goal in injury time. Michael Owen, now at Newcastle, is recalled. An uncharacteristically quiet game from Frank Lampard.

EFFORTLESS ENGLAND SLAUGHTER BENIGHTED BRAZIL LIKE FILTHY PIGS IN THE NIGHT 1-1

Reasonable people agree that the South Americans are a pretty extraneous shower, in the main. Were South America as a whole to sink into the sea - preserving, God willing, the precious Falkland Islands - I doubt that anyone would miss it, especially now that we have the recipe for refried beans. Fry them once – fry them again. Serve. Well done, that continent. Bally simple, really. However, having owned several mines and coffee planta-tions in the country, I must admit that I have harboured a modicum of affection for the Brazilians. They are a toothsome people. In my employ, they were paid a dollar a month, but being so happy and carefree, I believe they bundled together these excess dollars into a paper football, which they kicked about on the beach. Happy people. Indeed, I once owned one of them as a pet. Unfortunately, he started to demonstrate sullen tendencies and when I caught him attempting to smuggle a nut out of my mansion, secreted beneath his lower lip, I was forced to admin-ister him a thrashing and release him back into his habitat. Since then, I have learned to keep a weather eye on the beggars. In the glint of the eye of that fellow Ronaldinho every time he stepped up to take a free kick, I recognised the balefulness with which they habitually regard their European superiors and benevolent exploiters.

Of course, this night was all about the inauguration of the "new" Wembley, taking the place of the old. We shall all remember where we were when the Twin Towers fell, one of the keynote events of the new century, as the former stadium was demolished. And, for sure, in marking that day, we shall at least get the day and the month in the correct order. (memo to our former colonial subjects: November 9, 2001 passed entirely without incident. Please correct accordingly on all public monuments, souvenir mugs, etc).

There were many talking points tonight, not least of which was the recall of young Michael Owen. It has been kind of our Geordie cousins, from "hooway" up North, to look after little Mr Owen during his two year convalescence, during which he has made a few token runouts for the team in return for his real business of recovering to play for England. Not since they hanged those monkeys they mistook for French spies have they so effectively proven their patriotic mettle. We all looked on with bated breath, fingers crossed that Owen would survive the national anthems without sustaining an injury; this he did, to his enormous credit. The Brazilians, amusingly, not only have their own footballing Federation but their own national anthem. This, England's supporters were forced to endure stoically, despite its resemblance to the score of one of Mozart's lower farces and its longitude, which was such that I was half expecting an intermission midway through its performance.

The anthems over, and England's dominance established, there came the quaint and arguably irrelevant ceremony of the playing of the game itself. The Brazilians play, it is said, to the rhythms of the samba; we of England, however, play to the rhythm of "God Save The Queen", albeit rendered at 78 rpm, especially in the first few minutes of a fixture. The early moments were as predicted; the Brazilian players caressed and fondled with the ball in a manner so sexual, so obscene that it is surprising that a member of the constabulary did not intervene and escort the offenders off the pitch with a view to their appearing before a Vine Street magistrate, like one of those streaker fellows. The Brazilians did make some impertinent sallies forward but these were suppressed by Ledley King, who, I am informed, comes from a family of negroes. Why the fellow in the sheepskin coat employed to commentate for the British Broadcasting Corporation did not inform us of this interesting fact, nor his effeminate Irish counterpart, I cannot imagine. As for England as a whole, their play reflected the sheer ruggedness and no-nonsense variety of our cuisine. Imagine a feast of bully beef, spam, jellied eels, pig's knuckles, eggs fried in lard, black pudding and bread and dripping. Yes, it was that delicate, that subtle, that appetising. Young Shorey at left-back particularly caught the eye. He looks set fair to follow in the tradition of Luke Young and Chris Powell in the pantheon of Great English Defenders.

The first significant incident of the game saw a benighted Brazilian blighter pull down one of our stout English forwards.

Had this been a competitive fixture, the fellow would have been booked. Had this been on one of my plantations, the fellow would have been tossed screaming into a crocodile river in just his trousers by four of my strawhatted hands. Then again, this all begs the question of whether England can truly be said to be in a "competitive fixture", since no nation on this earth possesses the fibre to be considered adequate competition against them.

The next incident saw the Brazilians claim a headed goal, ruled offside. However, the header came from one Gilberto Silva, so the goal would have in any case been awarded to England, since he plays for Arsenal Football Club. The goal would have been the property of UK Customs & Excise.

There were many notable figures in attendance at this fixture. Spectators included Claudio Ranieri, the comical little man who used to manage Chelsea; Victoria Beckham and her two sons; and Frank Lampard. There were some suggestions that the relative emptiness of the stadium at the beginning of the second half was due to this fixture being packed out by slobbering, parasitical, fat, corporate reptiles who are leeching the game dry and whose voracious, empty-headed, gormless greed will ultimately result in the extinction not only of football but of all that is true and beautiful about life on the very earth itself. However, it is clear that they only emerged slowly to their seats in the second half with some surprise – surprise that, given England's sheer supremacy in the first half, the referee had not simply called the fixture off and awarded it to England, to save the Brazilians further humiliation. Clearly, our South American near species-relatives were unused to playing in boots and were befuddled by the green surface, which they doubtless took to be some extraordinary surfeit of washed up seaweed. Hence their inferiority. It is all in the breeding. Look at the Brazilians. Take their names, something Mr Merk summarily failed to do on several occasions. "Kaka", their forward. "Dunga", their manager. These people are positively excremental.

Take, then, by contrast, our own captain and inspiration, John Terry. Clearly, so manful, so lacking in effeminacy is he, that he is descended entirely from men. I doubt there is a single female on either side of his family tree. A quite absorbing, if not engorging thought. And how appropriate it was that, on this night of nights, when David Beckham (whom Mr McClaren was as wise to include as he was previously to exclude) delivered a trademark, inch-perfect cross, it was our Mr Terry, England's most potent organ of delivery, who connected to make the net bulge in a manner that was almost tumescent. One took great heart too, during a period in the second half when England found themselves, so to speak, "on the back foot", that we had reinforcements at hand, true strength in depth. For when the garrison is beleaguered and the natives are on the attack, what could be of more comfort, the very equivalent of the rescuing cavalry's bugle cry, than to look to the touchline and see the numbers flashed up of Downing and Dyer?

If we have learned one lesson tonight, however, it is that we must review as a matter of urgency whether visiting foreigners, such as, in this instance, the Brazilians, should have their visas restricted to a strict 90 minutes. Clearly, by the 92nd minute, they had outstayed their welcome and ought to have been harried onto the back of their lorry, and then the boat, before they could cause further distress to the Host Nation. This diplomatic incident means that now, a quarter of a century after we gave Argentina a trouncing in the South Atlantic, we must once again dispatch the HMS Sheffield, Coventry, Birmingham, Aston Villa, Wigan, Tottenham, etc, to mete out the same treatment to their near-South American neighbours. Just rejoice at that news, just rejoice!

ENGLAND V ESTONIA (European Championship qualifier)
June 6, 2007

*Routine victory against hapless Baltic opposition. David Beckham's
rehabilitation continues apace.*

ELEGANT ENGLAND EFFORTLESSLY ELIMINATE EXCECRABLE AND EXCREMENTAL ESTONIANS 3-0

The Estonian team came into this fixture with a reputation
whipped up by some of the sporting correspondents for an
excellent and obdurate defence. I would recommend to those
journalists that they read their history books. "May God in
Heaven thee defend, My best, my dearest land!/May He be
guard, may He be shield", runs a line from their national anthem,
whose melody is shared, abjectly, like an outside lavatory, with
that of Finland. It is a credit to the England team and to their
collective bowel control that they did not fall about laughing and
soiling themselves as the Estonians mewled out this portion of
their anthem prior to kick-off. For God has either been remiss in
his duties or, far more likely, considers the Estonians one of his
more regrettable creations. For since the numerous invasions of
the Baltic tribes in the Iron Age, through variously to the
Germans during the Northern Crusades then subsequently the
Danes, the Swedes in the 16th century, the Russians in the 18th
and then Germany in their pomp during the 20th, the Estonians'
ability to defend has been called into question on countless
occasions. They have been tossed around like the strumpet of the
Baltics for country after country to have their way with them as
they please. No doubt today, were they of a mind to, the Belgians
could send a bicycle detachment across to Estonia armed merely
with peashooters and they would have command of all key
airports, TV stations and parliament within 24 hours. These
Estonians are a sallow, surly, grey-faced sub-people, whose

principal exports are forest pine cones, slurry, sludge, unwanted plastic sandals, gone-off root vegetables, rancid potatoes and third-hand underwear, I reliably tell myself.

Contrast that with proud, puff-chested John Bull, our English boys who lined up tonight in this "stadium", which doubtless doubles as a communal bath for Tallinn's citizens, filled to the brim once a month. Ne'er did we stoop beneath the foot of a proud conqueror and we had no intention of doing so tonight. We are a noble and aloof island people. Had Nature not provided a channel between ourselves and the continent, we would most certainly have dug one ourselves and made it a jolly sight wider to boot.

The game commenced at a cracking pelt, so much so, that the referee, Mr Gilewski of Poland (one of our own – good decision, UEFA) could scarcely keep pace. The Estonians wore blue and were reduced to a blue funk as Michael Owen failed only to connect with pinpoint David Beckham crosses because, by cruel accident of birth, he happened not to be a foot and a half taller. Ledley King scampered about helpfully, his negritude no impediment on the night, it is appropriate to say. Steven Gerrard burst forward once or twice – what a shame that association football rules churlishly require that players actually do something useful with the ball as well as burst forward once or twice, otherwise the outcome of this fixture could have been settled even earlier. Frank Lampard played like two men, or at least is taking on those dimensions. Some players can be so busy as to appear to be in two places at once; Lampard always appears to be in the same place, twice, which is still more extraordinary.

England were playing cultured football as only England can. One did not for a second think of some desperately backward, flintmongering fifth century Anglo-Saxon tribe spending five hours trying to push a square-wheeled vehicle made of rocks and twigs five yards. Mysteriously, despite a Beckham free kick which, to universal astonishment, went wide, England did not crown their beguiling performance with a goal. Shame, however, on those who cast an eye to manager Steve McClaren on the touchline, imagining him to be scanning the back pages of Championship Manager's Gazette looking for vacancies as assistant under-coach. For up popped chirpy cockney Joe Cole, slippery as a jellied eel, by jove me Guv'nor, doing a Lambeth Walk through the Estonian defence and popping it in the back of the perishing onion bag. (Ugh. Seppings! The spittoon.)

In the second half, it would have been no surprise to see the Estonians emerge in England shirts, having been pinned up against the wall at bayonet point in the tunnel and conscripted to the cause. Certainly, matters could have been thus expedited more speedily. However, we are no savage conquerors but Englishmen fair and true, Christian and comely. And so, we let them play on in their own shirts, doubtless the only shirts some of these players own, merely handing out to them a formal thrashing and a lesson in the art of crossing to a 7'4" man, which is always a useful one to have under your belt. David Beckham was the architect of both England's second-half goals. Who could have predicted, as he received the ball on the right wing, slowed up, stood on it, put his hand to his forehead and looked towards the penalty box, asked his caddy to fetch him boot no.6 from the dugout, put on said boot, took shape, aim and lofted the ball high and true into the box, that he was about to deliver a cross?

With England in such awesome and dominant form, and their victory in next year's Championships as inevitable as the eventual return of the Gold Standard, the EEC should do something useful for once in their lives and consider stepping in to cancel next year's tournament, with England declared winners in advance. For were England to go to Switzerland and Austria and deliver up a series of dazzling and imperial performances such as tonight's, there could only be one outcome – Europeans in their millions would follow the example of their Polish counterparts and flock to England in droves, by rail, fleet and autogyro, in the hope of finding housing and work here so that they could declare themselves ersatz Englanders, able to cheer like us for players of the calibre of Downing, Bridge, Dyer and our numerous Coles. Europe would be in danger of capsizing; men would have to be posted along the borders with bullhorns declaring, "Now see here! Go back to your own wretched countries. You're Spanish, you're Dutch, you're just going to have to put it up with it, I'm afraid. Now back on your boats!" Let us hope men at the civil service are at this moment ordering the requisition of sandbags, barbed wire, bayonets and Alsatians (not of the foreign but the better, canine variety) to repel this very real danger.

ENGLAND V GERMANY (Friendly)
August 22, 2007

Following his first defeat and his first home defeat, another first for Steve McClaren – his first defeat at Wembley, thanks to an uncharacteristic error by goalkeeper Paul Robinson. Kieron Dyer appears in an England shirt.

ENERGETIC ENGLAND WIN THE MASTER RACE BY TWO FURLONGS AGAINST GUTLESS GERMANS 1-2

Prior to the disaster they were instrumental in striking against Europe and the world in the middle of the 20th century, the Germans were every inch the paradigm of the modern, progressive state. They were at the forefront of civilisation, advanced in their social and political thinking, with strong, sympathetic links to similar nations such as the United Kingdom. Then, as their people were led astray by a collective madness, they were plunged into a dark age. I speak of 1945, and the Germany that has persisted to the present day - a nation of European Union wafflers, tree preservers, muddle-headed beatniks and Volkswagen drivers, of provocatively effeminate synthesizer collectives and decidedly low-quality disc jockeys, a nation whose sartorial sense, their byword during the 1930s and 1940s, has been reduced to the spectacle of grown men wearing mauve tanktops and bright yellow leggings in the shopping malls of Hamburg, a city which once marched to a prouder rhythm than its present day strains of DJ Jurgen And The Rock Till You Are Hot! Hi Energy Boom Boy Disco Club remix of "Bridge Over Troubled Water" by the semites Simon & Garfunkel.

I do not deny that Nazi Germany had its faults. I often felt that Herr Goebbels' boots were not buffed to the high shine that one desires in a man of his important standing, while the Horst Wessel Lied, while always spirited in its rendition, was insufficiently Wagnerian, to my mind, truly to pump the vital organs erect. However, if one really wants to take issue with the National Socialists, then one must deplore their choosing the Germans, the Germans, of all people upon whom to confer the status of the Master Race. For it is clear that, despite the Austrian Herr Hitler's best and laudable efforts, these people are no more the Master Race than they are the Master Comedians, or the Master Vegetarians, for that matter. This was the truth that would out in the end. Indeed, as they proved during the Visigoth era, when all it took for the Romans to drive them back into the forest was to catapult dead livestock in their general direction, they are really little more than a sort of Goat People, their propensity to sprout facial and cranial hair in all manner of absurd places and arrangements proving that they have yet to understand, as a species, that being hirsute brings with it responsibilities as well as privileges.

It is small wonder that we made such short work of them in the recent conflict of 1939-45. I must admit that, as a speechwriter for the late Winston Churchill, I regret that he chose his own, rather craven text - "we shall fight them on the beaches", and so forth - when addressing the nation through the medium of wireless. I should have preferred that he adhered to the text I set out for him myself, which ran rather more as follows: "People of Britain, I urge you to roll out the barrel, for a very straight-forward victory lies ahead. We shall win the Battle Of Britain with great ease, with a man with no legs leading the aerial charge, which is technically even better than beating them with two arms tied behind our backs. Yes, of course, the Germans will overrun those invertebrate pansies the Dutch, the French and the Poles, but then, let us face it, these are nations so depleted in testosterone that they envy the manhood of our own Dame Vera Lynn. And should the Germans dare to wade across the channel, their bumbling operatives will be driven back into the sea clutching their trouser seats crying "Hilfe! Hilfe!" in cracked, Teutonic falsetto wails at the first sight of our 80 year old Home Guard officers showing them a glint of their bayonet steel. So, everyone relax and tune into the Light Entertainment programme to hear "Snake Hips!" Lawson and his Syncopated Toetappers perform their own lively composition the "Golliwog Rag", while we win the war for fun." For that is, after all, very much the way things turned out.

As the teams lined up for the national anthems, I equally doubted not that this "friendly" would turn out similarly. The German team, an odd assortment of sizes which demonstrated, perhaps, the haphazard nature of their eugenic experiments in the 1940s, did not look sanguine. What a contrast with our own boys, who, in singing the praises of our own dear Queen, were in certain cases quite clearly having to contain their tumescence, such was the ardour of their monarchism and the thinness of their shorts.

The game commenced at a typically cracking pelt, with England as ever shrewdly electing to commit 80% of their energies into the first ten minutes of the game - the element of surprise, you see, a tactic first deployed in the late 1960s and for which England's groaning trophy cabinet is ample testimony. Within 15 minutes we were a goal up, Micah Richards (negro) passing to Frank Lampard who slammed past the German 'keeper. It is quite clear, that, like Herr Hitler in the last days of his Reich, Lampard lives in an underground bunker beneath the pitch, appearing at surface level occasionally and surprisingly before disappearing back down the hatch again to preserve his energies and take on his essential daily pie intake. Other performances caught the eye. Michael Carrick executed a series of exquisitely angled, side-footed deliveries which landed, with uncanny directness, at the ankles of the German centre backs or into the crowd, as if Mr Carrick had said to himself mentally, "Row H, seat 38" and supplied, with pinpoint accuracy. Never were the words, "pointless, ineffectual streak of spacewaste who never gets criticised because no major football commentator wants to be evicted from the arse of Sir Alex Ferguson" less appropriate. David Beckham, assuming the legs apart position in dead ball situations which announces to a fearful opposition, "You'll never guess what I'm going to do next", offered a 21-gun salute to all that is great about the English game, firing regularly and harmlessly into the air.

Germany scored twice, the first a typically shabby tactic, going behind the Maginot Line English keeper Paul Robinson had quite clearly established. This was not cricket and can therefore be erased from the blackboard. However, come the second half, and the Germans palpably quailed as England trundled onto their pitch their deadliest weapon, their code-breaker, their bouncing bomb, their Dresden destroyer, Kieron Dyer. One saw the German players blanche as he entered the field, with his formidable tally of "no goals yet but after 33 well-earned caps bound to score one soon, surely" carried like an emblem upon his shield. It was surprising that at this point there were not mass defections among the German team to the England cause, with their hapless centre-backs approaching Mr McClaren on their knees, hands clasped, pleading that they had only been obeying orders from the evil dictator Klinsmann.

I should like to conclude by commending the patriotism of our players, particularly the likes of Rio Ferdinand, who doubtless defied the wishes of his own, Scotch manager in his conspicuously arduous first-half efforts. His departure at half time with a "slight groin strain", which may in all possibility spell the end of his lucrative club career and see him end up running a public house or some such, suggests a player for whom a zealous "country before club" spirit has always been pre-eminent. There is about our boys a spirituality that no German, for whom the refrain "Deutschmarks Über Alles" is a watchword, will ever understand. They are Angles, and Angels also, with John Terry our very Gabriel, practically ethereal in his extraordinary indifference to cash.

ENGLAND V ISRAEL (European Championship qualifier)
September 8, 2007

A much-needed victory against Israel, with Wright-Phillips among the goalscorers, still leaves England in a precarious position in the group. Israel are very poor in front of goal. An England performance markedly low on uncharacteristic errors. Phil Neville brightens up the game with his red boots.

INCREDIBLE ENGLAND THRASH THE MISERABLE JEWISH HOUNDS 3-0

Some days prior to this fixture, I received upon a tray from my man Seppings a missive from the choirmaster of King's College, Cambridge, the great grandson of a Varsity colleague of mine. He had heard that I followed events in the world of association football closely, and was wondering if I might care to lick the end of my quill and inscribe a few elevating lines of verse which might galvanise and encourage the English team. These he would set to music and arrange for his young chorister charges.

They would then perform the arrangement at Wembley Stadium, prior to the anthems. I cannot recall in their entirety the lines which I duly composed, but I do recall the chorus, which, if trilled from the mouths of boy sopranos, struck me as especially poignant;

"Come away, England. Put them in a funk/Let's drown the Jews in English spunk!"

Unfortunately, Seppings was tardy in trundling into my chamber the television set, which bore the scrape marks of the six flights of stairs he had dragged it up from the cellar, where it is stored for shame between international fixtures. Faithful fellow – he croaked a deferential "thank you!" as I lacerated him with my riding crop for his sluggishness. And so, I missed what was doubtless a stirring performance of ethereal purity, tuning in only in time to witness the two teams taking to the pitch. Out strode England, avoiding the baleful eyes of their Hebrew adversaries, accompanied by fresh-faced, excited little mascots, including a young master Shaun Wright-Phillips. Imagine that small boy's feelings when he was informed that, owing to England's lengthy injury list, he would actually be starting the game! Every ten-year-old's dream come true.

The national anthems, as ever, marked the stark contrast between our English selves and our miserable, shiftless opponents. The Jewish anthem, unless my ear trumpet deceived me, consisted of nothing but a low, contemptuous series of "Boos", delivered collectively by the team and sections of the crowd. English supporters looked on in silent surprise and disgust – not least because of what the many thousands of Semite supporters, their tickets doubtless bought with the proceeds of usury, said of the treachery that exists within our British midst. The arrogance – see here, if you were God's chosen people, he would not have given you those noses, which in any other race would be held on with elastic.

As for the delivery of the British national anthem, well, goalkeeper Paul Robinson looked especially fervent in his desire to Save Our Queen – and save her he would, unless Her Majesty had the misfortune to be delivered to him via a slow backpass from Mr Gary Neville, but that is so unlikely a contingency we need hardly dwell upon it.

The game commenced, with England battering down Jewish resistance with some judiciously delivered 70-miles-per-hour forward passes from Steven Gerrard and some sterling work from young Micah Richards who, once Gary Neville passes his 40th birthday, will become a deserving fixture in the team. However, as they have shown previously, in the home tie and in tedious urban stand-offs during the recent hostilities in Europe, the Israelis are an unreasonably obdurate and resistant people, morbidly obsessed with their own survival. It would have been most instructive for them to stand back and admire an exhibition display of attacking football, particularly from Mr Emile Heskey, whose grace and acumen in front of goal is of the sort that renders words such as "arse", "cow's", "banjo", "a" "couldn't", "with", "hit" and "a", utterly superfluous. However, they proved recalcitrant and paid the price for their insolence when England opened the scoring, with of all people, our little mascot opening the account.

England excelled all over the park. Playing two Coles was a masterstroke, sowing seeds of confusion in the opposition. Rio Ferdinand, as ever, played with such assured confidence it was as if he was already thinking ahead to next Wednesday's game, or at the very least thinking ahead to what he might fancy for breakfast the following morning. Bacon. And eggs. Maybe poached eggs. Or boiled. Boiled is nice. With toasted soldiers. Only you mustn't over-boil the eggs for soldiers, otherwise the yellow bit doesn't go runny. And I don't like the bacon too crispy, either. Hate it when it's too crispy. Yeah. No good, that.

Actually, it's all a bit confusing, I think I'll have a bowl of All-Bran instead.

It was no surprise when England added further to their tally in the second half. The third goal, however, was marred by an obscene display of exaggeration and gross fabrication on the part of the Israelite goalkeeper – a display betraying certain tendencies that 20th century historians might do well to bear in mind when chronicling some of the more controversial events of the Second World War, as fancifully recalled by the Hebrews.

As the match drew to its conclusion, a number of English fans departed early. It was clear, however, looking at the number of unoccupied seats that, so confident were a larger number of English fans, they had elected to depart the stadium prior to kick-off. Very shrewd. Those who remained, however, were in for an added treat: Phil Neville and Andrew Johnson were introduced onto the pitch, solely for the purposes of knockabout entertainment, the former running around pointlessly in his red clown shoes, the latter engaged in the sort of amusing, bald-head slapping antics that were a staple of light entertainment until Political Correctness strangled comedy in the United Kingdom.

If one salient lesson emerges from this fixture, it is this. Given Israel's abysmal display in front of the English goal, the nuclear weapon they possess should be confiscated. It should be donated to some other country who might actually make some attacking use of it and, on the rare occasions when they did, didn't send the thing sailing calamitously over the target. For judging by their aim in front of goal tonight, were they to make good on a declaration to annihilate nearby Iran, it would be the schoolchildren of Malta who would be best advised to duck for cover and assume the squatting position under their schooldesks.

ENGLAND V RUSSIA (European Championship qualifier)
September 12, 2007

A Michael Owen brace and a stylish goal from Rio Ferdinand, taking up an advanced position, give England a deserved victory against a subdued and inhibited Russia.

INSPIRED ENGLAND FORCE RUSSIA'S RED BEAR INTO THE PINK TUTU OF TOTAL HUMILIATION 3-0

Watching the sallow, pockmarked whelps who made up the Russian team trudge disconsolately onto the field of their doom, mumbling consonant-laden imprecations under their breath, squirrel's tails sewn to their scalps in lieu of hair, my mind was transported back to the days of 1918 to 1921, when I served as a high-ranking volunteer for the White Army, fighting the Bolsheviks. As I and my detachment galloped about the countryside, putting village after village to the torch, so as to inculcate in the peasants the same fear and fealty the Bolsheviks themselves had hoped to inculcate by burning down those selfsame villages a fortnight earlier, I wondered about the Russians. Looking into their faces as we ransacked their possessions, slaughtered their livestock, made a pyre of their thatched dwellings, forced their elders at bayonet point to do clog dances for our amusement, quaffed their vodka and had our way, one by one, with their rosy-cheeked daughters, there seemed to be an unaccountable air of resigned melancholy about them – as if they were determined to be miserable. What is it with you abject potato-people, I wished to bellow at them. Why don't you pull your socks up? But, of course, such words cut no ice with the Russians, since only a few, select members of the Soviet High Command had access to socks in those days, and even some of them had to share.

Today, of course, thanks to that famous fit of geopolitical common sense back in the late 1980s, when the red flag was lowered and the white flag raised in its place, Russia is to some extent "back on track". They even have the economic equality of

which Comrade Lenin dreamed. 80% of the country's assets are divided equally among 20 chosen oligarchs; the remaining 20% (potatoes, beetroots, some plastic shoes, second-hand pieces of string, flared jeans with the words "I GIVE MY HEART ELTON JOHN" embossed upon the trouser seat) are shared out equally among the rest of the people.

And yet, despite all this, there is something about the Russians which makes the lip curl scornfully. Take the names of their players – indeed, the referee, a Swede, should have taken the entire Russian team's names for clearly staggering onto the field without having had a wash. "Arshavin"? "Zhirkov"? These were not names, these were obscenities, calculated to offend their gracious hosts. No doubt if "Fuckov", "Cuntmunchev" and "Shitalloveryourfaceako" had been fit, they would have been selected also.

The Russian national anthem, we were informed, was the shortened version. This was a mercy, for the full version, I am told, lasts for an entire winter. It was played across No Man's Land during the Second World War in order to sap the spirits of German frontline troops as the cold set in. They were the lucky ones; German soldiers who were captured were forced to read Russian novels, unabridged, until they could bear it no longer ("Ilyich, come quickly, Grandfather has hanged himself in the barn!") and expired of sheer depression and tedium.

As for the English national anthem, our players, sadly, restricted themselves also to the abbreviated version. I, for one, could cheerfully have listened to several more verses intoned without confusion by Rio Ferdinand, word for word, including the exhortation to Marshall Wade to crush the Scots. With the crowd still wanting more, however, the team cut short their rendition, to a sigh of regret around the stadium.

Manager Steve McClaren was justly praised for his courage and vision in adhering to the line-up who acquitted themselves so well in last Saturday's annihilation of the Jews. There was none

of the air about our manager, to quote the writer of light prose PG Wodehouse, "of an inexpert conjuror whose trick has succeeded contrary to his expectations", or of a clueless, spineless gingerbread man tossed randomly onto the shores of good fortune by the tempestuous ocean of chance.

England's first-half performance was a masterclass in spunk and how to discharge it, frequently and with gusto. It was a veritable Charge of the Light Brigade, with John Terry riding high in the saddle, pumped, engorged, stiffening, erect, throbbing, moaning, groaning, surging, thrusting, slapping, exhorting, thrusting, and thrusting again . . YES! – a fine example to all young schoolboys watching. The Russians scattered in his wake, in a manner that struck me as reminiscent of peasants suffering the administrations of the White Army. Upfront, they were miserably ineffective. Small wonder that many Russians are wistful for the days of Stalin – there, at least, was a man who, when faced with his rivals and opponents, wasn't afraid to shoot.

England were a deserved two-nil up at half time and added to their tally after the break. All performances caught the eye. If the newspapers do not award Ashley Cole a 10/10 for his flawless display - which contained not one hint of a self-serving, luxury-addicted, poisonous, greedy little tosspot whose complacency and arrogance are in danger of eroding what skills and pace and commitment to the game he once had – then I should not be surprised if he almost crashes his car when the news is conveyed to him. However, this match truly belonged to Steven Gerrard. Small wonder that the homosexual-sounding Irishman employed by the British Broadcasting Corporation lavished him with praise, for his every move merited comment. Gerrard picks up ball in midfield, surges forward in search of glory despite other options being available, is picked off by Russian defence who swiftly counterattack. Hoorah! Gerrard makes surging run into penalty box, is shrugged off by Russian defence as he falls over own feet, Russians exploit gap in midfield to counter-attack dangerously. Hurrah! Steven Gerrard picks up ball 20 yards out, shoots and blasts against the window of one of the corporate boxes high up in the stands. Hoorah! Steven Gerrard stands, hands on hips, looking Gerrard-like, doing nothing. Hoorah! Steven Gerrard hoists the ball high up field with hope in his heart that, who knows, it might end up vaguely near an English player or at the very least an English ball-boy. Hurrah! Steven Gerrard exhorts his teammates with a "C'mon! Run! Kich it! Eh? Eh? Run! Kich? Kich and run! Eh?" Hoorah!

As the final whistle blew and Guus Hiddink was summoned from his dugout to sign the treaty acknowledging defeat and surrender, one could be well satisfied with another superlative England display - one which reflects well upon manager Mr McClaren, who is to be commended not just for his courage but for bringing a promising crop of English players through into the first XI, something increasingly uncommon in the modern game. He is also to be congratulated for his second-half tactical switch – dropping Michael Owen back to midfield and moving Rio Ferdinand to centre forward, a move which paid the dividends only he anticipated. This was a fine, youthful outfit, doing a good job in keeping the berths warm for the likes of Hargreaves, Gary Neville, Kieron Dyer, David Beckham, Paul Mariner, Warren Barton, all of whom will surely be back in the team once they have got over the after-effects of injury, old age and irrelevance.

If this fixture had an instructive, historical, geopolitical purpose, and it surely did, it was to scotch the bewilderment among military historians as to why Russia was allowed to expand its Empire during the 20th century, while England stood and did nothing. Why didn't we simply pop over there with a couple of regiments, march into Red Square, backed up with a couple of gunboats stationed offshore, surround the Kremlin and threaten its occupants with a bayonetting if they did not come out with their hands above their hats? The answer is simple. What in Heaven's name would we want with this bally, benighted place, unless one wanted an infinite supply of stewed cabbage, malfunctioning smelting compounds and bizarrely prolific serial killers? We have Middlesbrough, why would we need Omsk?

HUGH MCLAUGHTON, BROADSHEET CORRESPONDENT

21ST CENTURY BUTTERCUP GIRLS NO MATCH FOR IRON MEN OF YORE

Recently, I was taken to task by a certain lady, a female, so to speak, of the opposite gender, who, her femininity and womanhood notwithstanding, has been appointed to write for the sports pages, a decision which, in the light of her sex (I should point out that the lady in question is a woman) I would venture to say I find intriguing. She was upbraiding me for having shown no interest whatsoever in my columns in women's football. I stood up from my typewriter and rejoined that on the contrary, in this modern jet age, I confined myself exclusively to correspondence upon women's football, or certainly women as those of a more hard-bitten and Caledonian bent would have it. I referred her to this, my recent report, upon the match between the women of Chelsea and the women of Man Utd in the season's "curtain raiser" (or should that be "petticoat raiser"?) to the new season, the Community Shield.

One wonders what the players of yore, the likes of Bill Shankly, Jock McAustere, Dougie McGarraharragger, would have made of squealing, pirouetting damsels like Ms Christine Ronaldo? They would have had them on the pitch and then had them after the match, in the ginnel between the gas works and the glue factory, had their Presbyterian principles not precluded sexual intercourse with effeminate footballers upon the Sabbath. Sad times indeed in which a Wayne Rooney is upheld as some paragon of doughty manhood. For regarding his countenance, I recall manlier-looking creatures than he twirling their parasols as they ambled down Edinburgh's fashionable Craggie Parade, taking in the shop window displays and their wares of lace, finery, fancy goods, pink bottles of scented essence of pansy and suchlike.

This was supposed to be a sporting contest in the old, Corinthian school, with former enmities laid aside and camaraderie established among true men, blasted in the furnaces and smelted in the ovens, as so many able, hardy young Scotchmen quite literally were in the country's industrial pomp, and glad of the honest day's work. But what do the likes of Josephine Mourinho, reared by olive-tanned women more familiar with girdles than girders in the manless nation state of Portugal, know of such traditions? For true sportsmanship, one must cast one's mind back to the years surrounding World War II. One thinks of a man like Reginald Ramsbottom. Like so many brave young men of those trying times, he lost a limb in conflict – as a player with Derby, in a midfield collision with Preston North End's tigerish midfielder Willie Aird, in a 1937 Challenge Cup quarter-final. This did not hinder him from attaining a distinguished wartime record, as one of Monty's "Desert Rats". At the height of tensions in North Africa, it was Ramsbottom who hopped out of his base camp, over enemy lines as night stole over the sand dunes, to surprise a tentful of Rommel's key aides to whom he administered individually the benefit of a brisk bayoneting before hopping back to camp, downing a tin mug of tea, then scoring three goals in a kickabout with a scratch team of local sandboys, his team prevailing 13-6. Hard indeed for the likes of a Rio "Ooh, I've just been pushed over by a foreign girl" Ferdinand to comprehend such mettle, such valour. Ramsbottom was second to none in his disdain for the "sausage scoffers".

One recalls the occasion when the England team were obliged to stand and deliver the Nazi salute before an international fixture with the German national team. I think not of the 1938 fixture but another, much forgotten by football's chroniclers, in 1946. Ramsbottom was briefly caretaker manager, and a friendly fixture had been arranged between England and Germany. Some considered the fixture ill-advised in the light of recent events, but not Ramsbottom. Though instrumental in the victorious outcome of the British Empire, he considered it only fit and respectful to honour the recently vanquished. And so, as the players lined up, and with the national anthems concluded, he strode out from the dugout and, in an impromptu gesture, bellowed to his players, "Three cheers for the Nazis! Hip-hip, HOORAY!" and with each "Hooray", he thrust his right arm rigid and diagonally aloft, bidding his team to do the same. Which they did, registering, it must be said, some consternation. The German team, too, history must record, appeared embarrassed also, for they misunderstood the workings of the British mind. Yes, their nation languished in the abjection of defeat on the battlefield – but they had put up a pretty stiff fight and Ramsbottom was determined to commend them for that. Of course, today's "politically correct" brigade would disparage Ramsbottom for his actions – but then, they understand little of blood, honour, or soil. Or girders.

What has all of this to do with the game? Very little, sadly. What was the score? I know not. What happened during the game? I do not know, I watched it not. Suffice to say that the Manchester United team over whom "Sir" Alice Ferguson presides would not be fit to be bridesmaids at the weddings of the eleven men and true of United's vintage line-up of 1902, whose hard-fought 13-13 draw with the Associated Draymen's Works XI in the old Third Division North-West remains their proudest moment.

ENGLAND V ESTONIA (European Championship qualifier)
October 13, 2007

Comfortable home win for England, sealed in the first half with the assistance of an own goal. All that's required now to qualify for Euro

2008 is to beat Russia. A fine day for English sport, with the rugby union team also prevailing against France in Paris.

ALMOST EDIBLY EXCELLENT ENGLAND ELIMINATE EXECRABLE ESTONIANS 3-0

As part of my research for this vital fixture, upon whose outcome the prestige of the English race was as ever staked, I took in an extensive survey of what laughably passes for Estonian culture. This included the music of a certain Mr Arvo Pärt, unutterable, liturgical bilge of the worst stripe whose remorselessly maudlin drones speak volumes about the vodka-soaked despair in which the Baltic states marinate. It also meant subjecting myself to the novels of a certain Emil Tode. I shall not elaborate upon his 1993 work, Piiritik, the tale of an Estonian on the run from a crime committed in Paris, nor dwell on its disgusting, homosexual overtones. I would merely counsel that is not the sort of book you should allow your wives and manservants to read, nor for that matter your mistress or even the scullery maid you once pursued across the grounds of your estate on horseback, brandishing your riding crop with lascivious intent. Hardly the sort of book at all. However, it is said that the novel represents, in some metaphorical way, the Estonians' desire to pursue a sense of their own wider European-ness, to become players on a more international stage and thereby somehow better themselves. Such aspirations must be stoutly resisted. There is a reason that England is a country and Estonia is a state. This is because the Estonians are in a frightful state. An absolute shambles, in fact: a people who have as a whole yet to recover from the passing of the Bronze Age. These people eat cabbage for breakfast. Cabbage and toasted soldiers is no way to fortify yourself for the rigours of the day. This, then, was more than an association football match. It was a war between eggs and cabbages, both boiled.

As England's men and negroes lined up, shoulder to shoulder

for the national anthems, it was clear that they were aware of what was at stake. The away fans, the vast majority of whom had paid for their tickets through several months of manual labour, prostitution, etc, doubtless prayed to their own Estonian God (a fabled, forest creature, half man, half goat) that their miserable collection of would-be Nordic human jetsam would by some miracle carry the day. Thankfully, their rogations were in vain as the English God, to whom Steven Gerrard and co bellowed exhortations that he devote his entire attention to ensuring the personal safety and longevity of Her Majesty, had other ideas. A comely female was trafficked in to sing both anthems but there could be no doubt as to which would go heeded.

The game began at a typical, thunderous pace. It is only a shame that England were not able to mount their charges on the Estonian goal on horseback, for such are the pernickety rules and regulations of UEFA's bureaucracy in these equine matters. No matter, for the midget Wright-Phillips soon opened the tally with a goal of which all extremely short people can be proud. Minutes later, it was Wayne Rooney's turn. The whole country was willing him to score and, in the shape of the Estonian team, it was as if he had had mustered before him by well meaning stag night chums a bevy of glamorous Grandmothers, all rouge lipstick and fishnet tights, all eager to pass on to him the benefits of fifty or sixty years of sexual dalliance. He could not fail to score. Surely could not fail to score. And score he did, his effort just the right side of flaccid to register as adequate. Now, all England could relax, its talisman potent once more.

England's tally was also augmented, somewhat obsequiously, by an Estonian defender, a clear attempt to curry favour with the immigration authorities and assist his application to reside permanently on this sceptr'd isle in some sort of carwashing capacity. It will cut no ice, however. He will be herded onto a chartered fishing boat come Sunday evening along with his teammates, for the 38-hour journey, via the North Sea, back to the benighted Baltics.

Come the second half and England were able to relax sufficiently to put on a comedy show of sorts for the Wembley
faithful, in the absence of any threat from their already subju-
gated opponents, whose dreams of racial improvement lay about
them in tatters. Paul Robinson did an uproarious turn, worthy of
any music hall revue, as a "Butterfingered Northerner" when he
deliberately fumbled a long range shot from the Estonians
("Oooh eckers peckers, like, I'm all of a fritter, 'ey oop, mother,
where's me ukulele?" and so forth). And Steven Gerrard, upon
the award of a free kick, took the opportunity to try out his
sketch, "Inexplicably Deified, Puddingheaded Scouse Twat
Sprays Football About As Wildly As He Sprays His Phlegm".
Fans duly rolled in the aisles. The only surprise was to see Frank
Lampard emerge onto the pitch as a substitute. I had assumed he
had been on the pitch the entire game, putting in a performance
typical of the player. So exhausting was this rollercoaster of a
fixture that I fear I may briefly have dozed off. However, I awoke
in time to see late England substitute Jonny Wilkinson put a long
range effort unluckily just over the bar, though thankfully this
did not affect the triumphant outcome against the men in blue.

Two things emerge from this fixture. The first is that, for the
purposes of geopolitical simplification, this 3-0 score should
count next Wednesday against Russia also, since to most of our
minds, Russia and Estonia and all the various other spurious
satellite states arrayed like tugboats across Eastern Europe are
pretty much of a muchness. If, in return, Russia wished to re-
occupy Estonia by force of invasion, that need hardly put out the
FA or Mr McClaren. A little quid pro quo of this sort is quite
harmless.

The second concerns John Terry. England's captain, hero and
inspiration by dint of his erect carriage and upright bearing was
unavailable on the pitch today, thanks to a variety of injuries
which make one think, and think hard, of the martyr St Sebastian.

However, do not suppose that he would not have exhorted his men on in a address in the dressing room beforehand. I have composed his probable speech. "Men!" he would have shrieked. "The hour is at hand. An hour for men! For Englishmen, engorged with the thought of the tussle ahead! The physical tussle, the close grapple with the swarthy, hairy foe! Let us therefore grease ourselves for battle! Let us oil our torsos like men! Men! Let us gird and lubricate our loins in preparation! Like men! Men! Men upon Men! Men, to the hilt! Upright and pumping!" Ah, yes – the stiffening, the summoning up of the blood, which causes a tingling that spreads as far away as the Northern extremities right down to the Cotswolds.

ENGLAND V RUSSIA (European Championship qualifier)
October 17, 2007

Perturbation for Steve McClaren as The Russians water their synthetic pitch surface prior to kick-off. Wayne Rooney scores but then, with uncharacteristic impetuosity, gives away a penalty. Russia equalise, then pull ahead with a second goal from Pavlyuchenko. England's fate is no longer in their own hands.

EXEMPLARY ENGLAND ROUT RISIBLE AND RANK RUSSIANS 1-2

Upon arriving in Moscow, and instructing the porter to fetch hither from the airport the crate containing all my personal effects including my portable lavatory, my stereopticon and my man Seppings, my nostrils wrinkled at a particularly foul bouquet. This pervaded not just the lobby area but the city as a whole. I initially thought nothing of it. This is, after all, Russia, the eighteen-stone, shambling halfwit with a rope around its neck of Europe, a nation barely erectus in evolutionary terms, where correct personal hygiene remain as wistful and elusive a prospect as does that of telepathic communication to us in the West. However, upon entering the stadium and witnessing the pitch being sprayed with copious fountains of water, I realised what had happened. Quite clearly, strict water rations had been in operation throughout the city for a month now, with bathing temporarily banned and Muscovites risking the withdrawal of their potato privileges if they breached the order. The gallons withheld would be deployed instead in a shabby attempt to wash up their mighty opponents England, fair footballing means being, of course, out of the question for these sub-people.

If the Soviets imagined for one moment that this tactic would work, they reckoned without two things. First, every man-jack of the England team would play on any surface for their country. They would play on red hot coals if necessary, and even on a pitch strewn with tin tacks (a prospect of which our Arab opponents in particular have a peculiar horror). Secondly, they forget that after ten minutes of Steven Gerrard's Liverpudlian exhortations, any pitch upon which England play is generally reduced to a similarly soggy state.

The national anthems of course, sorted the Gods from the goats. Unconscionably, the Muscovites booed our own, dear anthem and its lusty rendering. How I wished to pass among these odious curs on my white steed, brandishing a mace. However, I was not altogether surprised at this antipathy. My man Seppings's lacklustre deportment as I bade him stand for the anthem, though inexcusable, could be accounted for by his having been beaten up violently by locals earlier in the day. He had been walking around Red Square at my bidding, clad in a pair of union jack combinations which he was breaking in for me, worn outside his pinstripes to improve their elasticity. As for the Russian national anthem, it was inglorious in its sentiments. One couplet, roughly translated, reads: "May the annual regional crop reports be favourable/And the Secretary General's sister-in-law secure a dacha adequate for the needs of herself, her mother and her several spaniels." Hardly the stuff to set the loins pumping. To print the surnames of our opponents would probably to be in breach of the Obscene Publications Act. (Arse Shaving? Minge Grazing? Cock Gobbling? These are not names, they are criminal offences, surely!) So to avoid confusion, for the purposes of this report, I shall simply refer to each of the Russian players as "Ivan".

There was much talk about the plastic pitch, of course. Again, those familiar with the Russian nation will be aware that there is little or no grass left in the country, since most of it was eaten in desperation by starving peasants and citizenries during the Grand Famine of 1917-33, the Great Famine of 1935-56 and the Tremendous Famine of 1958-1979. That this would be of no consequence was evident as the game began, at full tilt. As is so often the wont of our opponents, they "passed" the ball about to one another somewhat effeminately, like slices of angel cake on doilied plates among women at an informal light opera recital. Ivan to Ivan, across to Ivan, who passes back to Ivan, who puts a through ball to Ivan. None of that for England. We are men; we do not pass the ball to one another, we shoot it at one another, as Gerrard demonstrated when he almost took Wayne Rooney's head off with one such thunderously virile delivery.

This was exemplary fare. Had Michael Owen been on the pitch tonight, he would have been proud of the efforts of his colleagues. Tennyson would have been moved to write poems about them. Defensively, England were particularly strong. Watching Sol Campbell move was as impressive as watching a giant oil tanker in the stately process of a three point turn. Watching Rio Ferdinand was like watching a man watching said oil tanker turn, mouth agape, utterly absorbed ("Cor . . . . . . look at that . . . . blimey . . . ."). As for Paul Robinson, no doubt he took to the pitch buoyed by words of encouragement from manager Mr McClaren and enjoying the full confidence of his teammates. It was certainly not as if assistant manager Terry Venables had taken the players aside just as both Robinson and McClaren had left the dressing room and said, "Right. Ignore everything that cretinous fucking heap of carrot gratings just said. We'd be better off with a fucking scarecrow planted between the pegs than that Northern lummox. Why he doesn't . . . anyway, what I basically want you to do, right, is play like we don't have a fucking goalkeeper. Got it? Because we fucking haven't, basically. Understand? Got it? Joleon? Good. Stevie? Good. Micah? Good. Sol? Good. Rio? Rio? Rio! RIO!!"

With England comfortably ahead at half time, arrogance, lack of concentration and complacency certainly did not set in come the second half. Granted, Joe Cole could be spotted at one point out on the wing on his mobile phone to the airline making sure he got a window seat for the flight home and then to his agent to discuss a photography shoot for GQ, but these were quite sensible and necessary calls and in no way detracted from his 100%, all guns blazing commitment to the cause.

Indeed, what happened next was an unwarrantable travesty. Wayne Rooney simply tapped on the shoulder of Ivan, doubtless to ask him what the international telephone code was, so that he could put in a quick call to his fiancée to say he would be home in 90 minutes, so put a roast in the oven. Whereupon Ivan collapsed in a heap and the referee awarded a penalty which Ivan duly converted. Ivan added a second moments later.

Thankfully, with just minutes to go, the mood not just of the game but of watching nations was transformed utterly. The clouds appeared to part in anticipation, while a hush descended across the stadium. Ivan looked worriedly at Ivan. For, on the touchline, an official lifted a board. The moment was upon us.

Frank Lampard was about to enter the field of play.

And, lest we forget, Stewart Downing.

Panic duly ensued. Ivan's shorts turned moist, brown and pungent, as did Ivan's. For the game was surely up, now. And, indeed it was, a few moments later. The final whistle blew, with Lampard having distinguished himself by placing a perfectly weighted ten-yard ball precisely equidistant between two of his own players, to the waiting feet of a visibly disconcerted and fatally demoralised Ivan.

As I took to my bed that evening, with Seppings standing upright and respectfully at my bedside, with my personal bed bucket over his head to block out the light as he tried to sleep, the ramifications of this fixture made themselves clear to me. First, an FA representative should be dispatched to London Zoo with a tape measure to make a random selection. The next day, the press should be gathered at Soho Square for an official announcement. Whereupon, a fucking chimp in a little fucking made-to-measure fucking blazer and fucking tie should be wheeled out on a pair of fucking roller skates and fucking announced as the new fucking England manager. A fucking chimp. This, I should make clear, is no reflection on the sterling efforts of Mr McClaren. It would simply point up the fact that so great, so good is this England team that they no more need to be "managed" than they do, in most cases, need to be spoonfed their daily bowl of porridge. The very appointment is an affront to their innate sense of comradeship and tactical awareness. It should therefore be made a mockery of.

Second, given the possibility that some FIFA jobsworth might pedantically disregard the entire moral tone of this fixture and award the match to Russia on the spurious technical point that they scored more goals, the match be replayed – but this time England choose the liquid substance with which the pitch should be doused prior to the game. I would suggest a substance that is viscous, fertile and adhesive – that would not only slow up the Russians' sneakily effeminate passing game but also prevent any unexpected bounces of the ball the like of which are so prone to upset Paul Robinson. We'd need gallons of the stuff – fortunately, my man Seppings has been hard at it down at the stables, procuring the substance from several of my best horses with a busy hand, the hoofmarks on his chest testimony to their only occasional reluctance to oblige.

ENGLAND V AUSTRIA (Friendly)
November 16, 2007

Austria host England in a somewhat tepid friendly in preparation for the last group fixture against Croatia. A Crouch goal settles matters, but the performance is marred by Michael Owen picking up an uncharacteristic injury.

ADMIRABLE ENGLAND ANNIHILATE ABJECT AUSTRIANS 1-0

Ah, Austria, Austria, a country for which, I concede, I harbour a certain fondness, even admiration of a qualified sort. One notes with approval, for example, the way in which they emerged from the privations and, dare one say, needless enmity of World War II, going about their post-war business as if nothing had happened, which is all to the good. I spent some pleasant years during the 1970s away from England, when the takeover of my local grocer's store by a certain, shall we say, gentleman, bore out predictions made by Mr Powell of the nation's descent into a foaming Tiber. I resided in most agreeable lodgings in the elevated town of Genau between the years 1973 and 1976, with commanding views of the wending Danube, detached from the cares of the world, tended to by a rosy-cheeked, white haired landlady Frau Ulrich, in an idyllic, gabled, one might say gingerbread-style dwelling in Adolf Hitlerstrasse, just off the town square.

One admires, also, the way in which these people played their part in the running of the Austro-Hungarian Empire, in an accord reached in 1867 – a power-sharing arrangement, so to speak. I am not aware of the historical niceties - I leave those to experts like Mr Irving - but it would appear that the Austrians ran the Empire on Mondays, Wednesdays and Fridays, the Hungarians Tuesdays, Thursdays and Saturdays with alternate arrangements for Sundays. How efficiently, one feels, this could have worked, had Herr Hitler and Mr Churchill reached an accord in 1940. We could have had the Anglo-German Empire, one which would have made our American friends blink and other continents, particularly the lower down ones, quail. Imagine: Mondays, Wednesdays and Fridays would have seen Herr Hitler in charge, with compulsory eurythmics for the ladies while some of the Chancellor's burlier henchmen were dispatched to resolve certain pressing questions; meanwhile, on Tuesdays, Thursdays and Saturdays, it would have been compulsory beach-fighting (in case Ivan got any ideas) and enforced sterilisation of the working classes under the aegis of Mr Churchill, or, should he have happened to have been inebriated, his butler. There would have been no need for the meddling little fool Clement Attlee, "The Backslider's Benefactor".

And yet, as so often, one's contemplation of alliances with our sausage-inclined racial equals run aground on the rocks of reality. One does wonder how robust their Empire really was when all it took was a Serbian halfwit with a popgun to bring it collapsing around their ears in a heap. These people, for all their umlauts, mountain lodges and lurches to the Far Right are, in essence, God's first, botched effort at making Germans. Where once they strutted with virility and mastery around the globe, this nation that once produced the world's greatest writers, composers, philosophers and dictators must now endure the ignominy of wearing tight leather shorts and slapping each other's backsides at the toss of a coin of a tourist. One is no racial theorist, but perhaps this is due to their too-close proximity to peasant nations like modern Hungary, and the deleterious effect on their stock of the stench of boiled cabbage, unwashed armpits and rusty three-wheel vehicles wafting across their borders.

And sure enough, as they lined up in the Horst Wessel Stadium, English pride had prevailed already against the pitiful Schnitzels in red, who already had the look of men whose only future prospects lay in the domain of mutual anus-slapping. The national anthems demonstrated that England's fervent, bellowed desire that our Queen be saved from death at a too-youthful age were far more likely to be fulfilled than were that Austrians' wish stated in their own anthem, albeit subtextually, that the price of veal remain stable in the forthcoming fiscal year. As far England's selection – Beckham, Owen, Campbell – one only regrets Mr McClaren's forward-looking boldness was not so bold as to see him include Bryan Robson and Paul Mariner.

With England having attained an unassailable 1-0 lead at half time, the second half might as well have consisted of England's eleven emerging in top hat and spats, running through a medley of Cole Porter and Noel Coward numbers. David Beckham playfully and good-naturedly teased the Austrian's first defender at set piece situations by pinging the ball deliberately against his head, time and time again, for fun. Clearly, his time spent in the United States among the vaudeville and Nickelodeon stars has been to the good. Mr Dead-Eye we are used to, but this was an altogether new character - Mr Chortles.

And yet, tragedy struck when the normally indestructible Michael Owen had his thigh rent asunder as, with Austrian defenders clearly encroaching within his ten-yard personal space, he shaped to shoot and, as one would under that sort of strain, became injured. Not even the betting circles of which young Michael prudently steers clear would have invited wagers on such an unlikely outcome. Still, since all it would have taken in any case to bring about Austria's utter defeat this night was to field one Serbian idiot – and frankly, as recent history tells us, such a person would not be hard to find - Owen's departure was of no matter.

This fixture was of enormous significance, as it cut out the various middle men. This game was against the hosts of the 2008 European Championships, the very hosts. It was, therefore, to all intents and purposes, the European Championship final. Be under no illusion about that. It would therefore make sense, and save a good deal of time-wasting next summer, if the trophy were awarded to England on the basis of this hard-fought and well-merited victory. Were Mr Sepp Blatter to clamber upon Princess Anne at some sporting function and ride her around the room like one of her horses, bellowing Swedish obscenities, he could not deliver a more coarse and calculated insult to the nation of England than were he to dare to refuse us the cup.

ENGLAND V CROATIA (European Championship qualifier)
November 21, 2007

Despite only requiring a draw to progress, England lose 3-2, crashing out as manager McClaren, from beneath his umbrella, looks on at an uncharacteristic display of fallibility and ineptitude.

Good evening. I should commence by introducing myself. My name is Seppings. I did have a Christian name – however, I fear I mislaid it around the time of the Boer War, when I first came into the employment of my current master. I further fear that, having lost consciousness midway through the first half of tonight's association football contest, he is unable to complete his customary report. He is prostrate upon his white tiger carpet and has turned a somewhat rich hue of blue. Given that he has failed to exhibit signs of breathing, or an active pulse for that matter, for some 80 minutes now, it might perhaps behove me to make a telephonic call to the Emergency Services. However, I know my master well and I believe that he would not wish me to attend to him, even in his dire and potentially fatal condition, before I had filed a report upon England's performance this night. I shall therefore dip quill in inkwell and attempt, as well as I can muster, to function as an ersatz scrivener in his stead and do my poor best to reflect the events of this evening's game as they happened, and, naturally, mete out to the English team the glory and tribute that is their due. My master did jot some notes as regards the national anthem. He recommended that the choice of the singer, a certain gentleman of pronounced pigmentation, was erroneous. That he went on to sing the Croatian anthem also, he opined, was proof that his papers be checked and that he be deported back to his country of origin, perhaps upon a boat containing fruits considered unfit for English consumption, for his gross treachery.

Anyhow, I shall try to be faithful to my Master's Voice; and, should I err or deviate, I trust I shall have a modicum of sympathy from those who witnessed this match. My report is as follows;

FOR FUCK'S SAKE, WAS THIS A FUCKING PITCH OR A FUCKING PADDYFIELD? YOU'D THINK, GIVEN THE FUCKING MILLIONS WE POOR FUCKING TAXPAYERS HAVE BEEN FUCKING PROPAGANDISED INTO COUGHING UP BY THE UNACCOUNTABLE, BLAZER-SUITED, RED-NOSED SIX-MAN COMMITTEE OF BEAK-WETTING CUNTS WHO LAUGHINGLY PASS FOR THE POWERS THAT FUCKING BE, AND GIVEN THAT THE FUCKING STADIUM WAS ABOUT SIX FUCKING YEARS LATE IN APPEARING, THEY COULD AT LEAST HAVE PROVIDED US WITH A PITCH THAT HAD A SLIGHTLY MORE ROBUST FUCKING CUNTING CONSTI-TUTION THAN A FUCKING CESSPIT!

ANYWAY, COME THE FUCKING GAME! RIGHT FROM THE FUCKING GET-GO THIS WAS SHITE PLAYING ON FUCKING

SHITE! THIS IS FUCKING CROATIA, A FUCKING NATION WHOSE FUCKING FLAG IS A FUCKING TABLECLOTH AND WE'RE FUCKING LETTING THEM CUT THROUGH US LIKE FUCKING MELTED BUTTERSHIT? OH, FUCK, THEY'RE NOT EVEN FUCKING TRYING, THEY'RE JUST PUNTING THE FUCKING BALL IN THE VAGUE FUCKING DIRECTION OF OUR FUCKING GOAL AND WOULD YOU BELIEVE IT, SCOTT FUCKING "WORK EXPERIENCE" CARSON, OUR FUCKWIT BUTTERSHIT-FINGERED KEEPER MAKES A FUCKING HASH OF IT AND NOW WE'RE EATING FUCKING CESSPIT FUCKING SANDWICHES! JESUS H CUNT!

OH MY FUCKING CUNTING CHRIST ALMIGHTY WILL YOU GET A FUCKING GRIP, YOU GQ-FILLING, PORSCHE-CRASHING, NIGHTCLUB-PROWLING, WAG-SLAVERING WANKERS! JOE TWATTING COLE! YOU'RE IN A FUCKING TEAM! STOP FUCKING DUCKING AND DIVING, YOU HORRIBLE LITTLE COCKNEY FUCKING WANKER, AND FUCKING PASS THE FUCKING BALL! CAMPBELL! YOU TURN SO FUCKING SLOW THEY SHOULD ATTACH FUCKING SIDELIGHTS TO YOUR FUCKING ARSE! WRIGHT-PHILLIPS! BASICALLY, YOU'RE TOO FUCKING SHORT! YOU HAVE A FUCKING SHORT PERSON'S FUCKING LOSER MENTALITY – BECAUSE FACE IT, SHORT PEOPLE ALWAYS ULTIMATELY FUCKING LOSE – AND IT FUCKING TELLS ON OCCASIONS LIKE THIS! OH, MY FUCKING GODCUNT, 2 FUCKING NIL? WHY DON'T THE FUCKING BACK FOUR JUST WEAR FUCKING BLUE BERETS AND JUST HAVE FUCKING DONE WITH IT? JUST LIE DOWN AND LET THE FUCKING CROATIANS DO WHATEVER THE FUCK THEY FUCKING TWATTING ARSEING WANT, THAT'S THE CUNTING SPIRIT!

SECOND HALF! FUCKING BECKHAM ON! IT'S FUCKING

COME TO THIS! IT'S LIKE WHEN THEY BROUGHT FUCKING BET LYNCH BACK TO FUCKING CORONATION STREET, IT'S THAT FUCKING DESPERATE! OH, RIGHT! PENALTY! WHAT, LAMPARD'S BEEN FUCKING PLAYING? DOING FUCKING WHAT? SUBMERGING YOURSELF IN THE FUCKING PITCH LIKE A FUCKING FROGMAN ONLY TO FUCKING POP UP WHEN THERE'S A FUCKING CHANCE FOR FUCKING GLORY? ALL RIGHT! 2-2!

FUCKING GERRARD, YOU PUDDING BOWL, FUCKING GUTS AND PRIDE AND PASSION AND PHLEGM-SPRAYING EPITOME OF ABSOLUTELY FUCKING EVERYTHING THAT IS FUCKING WRONG WITH THE PRESENT FUCKING ENGLAND SET-UP! YOU HAVE DONE NOTHING, REPEAT, FUCKING NOTHING OF ANY SHITTING USE ALL PISSING FUCKING NIGHT! IT'S THIS FUCKING SIMPLE! YOU CANNOT FUCKING PASS THE FUCKING BALL! IT'D BE AS EASY TO CATCH A FUCKING BULLET IN MID-AIR AS IT WOULD BE TO LATCH ONTO ONE OF YOUR SO-CALLED FUCKING PASSES! BEING PASSED TO BY YOU IS LIKE BEING FUCKED BY FUCKING SUPERMAN, THE FUCKING DISCHARGE PASSES RIGHT THROUGH YOUR FUCKING BODY AND SPLATS AGAINST THE FUCKING WALL AND THE POOR FUCKING DISCHARGEE BLEEDS TO FUCKING DEATH! YOU USELESS, POINTLESS SCOUSE CUNT! IT'S NO USE CHARGING RANDOMLY AROUND THE FUCKING PITCH LIKE FUCKING CORPORAL JONES, ENGAGE THAT FUCKING CAULIFLOWER FLORET OF YOURS THAT PASSES FOR A FUCKING BRAIN! NO, TOO FUCKING LATE, YOU'VE FUCKING LOST THE BALL IN FUCKING MIDFIELD FOR THE ONE HUNDRED AND CUNTING FIFTIETH TWATTING TIME, AND NOW IT'S 3-2 AND THAT IS FUCKING THAT!

AT LEAST ONE GOOD THING'S COME FROM THIS RANCID

COCK OF A FUCKING FIXTURE! THE FIRST IS THAT STEVE, FUCKING CARROT TOPPED CUNTMEISTER MCCLAREN NEEDS TO BE SACKED, NOT JUST FUCKING METAPHORI-CALLY BUT LITERALLY, SEWN IN A FUCKING SACK, LOWERED INTO A POOL AND SLOWLY NIBBLED TO DEATH BY FUCKING GOLDFISH, HIS OWN FUCKING GINGER CUNTING FUCKING SORT! STILL GLAD WE GOT A FUCKING ENGLISHMAN TO MANAGE THE FUCKING ENGLAND TEAM, EH? NEVER AGAIN! NEXT TIME A FUCKING ENGISHMAN IS DOWN THERE ON THE FUCKING TOUCHLINE HOLDING A FUCKING UMBRELLA, IT SHOULD BE OVER THE HEAD OF SOME FOREIGN CUNT WE'VE GOT IN AS MANAGER, WHO KNOWS WHAT THE FUCKING ARSEING CUNTING FUCK HE'S DOING!

ENGLAND V SWITZERLAND (Friendly)

February 6, 2008

New England manager Fabio Capello witnesses a satisfactory perfor-mance with goals from Jenas and Wright-Phillips. It is generally accepted and understood that England will not be participating in the forthcoming European Championships – but not universally.

EXCEPTIONAL ENGLAND ANNIHILATE CHEESE-DRINKING NEUTRAL MONKEYS 2-1

And so, we come to the Switzerland Question. What can be said, one wonders, of a nation whose patron saint is an alcoholic dog called Bernard, a nation who obdurately refuse to give back to certain German veteran acquaintances of mine, presently residing in Bolivia, the gold they stored there in good faith during the recent hostilities, and whose national anthem, essen-tially a yodelled recipe for fondue accompanied by cowbells, has presented the Coldstream Guards with such difficulty over the years when obliged to render it on state occasions? Certainly, they are a headstrong people – how else can one explain the rash decision of one of their regional districts, or cantons, the Appenzell Innerrhoden, to grant women the vote as early as 1990?

It was against such an impetuous and tricky opponent that our English men and true were pitted, in what constituted an important warm-up match for England's upcoming campaign in Euro 2008 – tonight, we would get a taste of what sort of opposition we can expect in that tournament. One surmises, however, after this performance, that we shall have little to fear. That the tournament will be played at all after this superlative victory is indicative of the petty bureaucratic pedantry of the European Union – the farcical notion that the continental nations enjoy parity with John Bull is, frankly, political correctness gone mad, incurred at the British taxpayer's expense. As a wise man once said: first, they straighten your bananas. Then, they measure them in centimetres. Then, they insist on Euro 2008 going ahead, despite the English team's manifest superiority. Then, they paddle across the continent, come ashore, moustaches glistening, armpits stinking, impregnate our daughters and insist on naming the offspring "Pierre".

It was in order to avert such a horrific prospect that this vital game was played. And, as the players lined up, in the countenance of Rio Ferdinand one palpably sensed the urgency of the occasion. In his furrowed brow one could track his stream of consciousness and, as sure as Prince Harry is the fruit of Prince Charles's loins, it was nothing like the following; " . . . . Playstation . . . . bling . . . .
. . . . merked, he he . . . . Playstation .
. . . .
. . . .
. . . . .Playstation . . . .
. . . . Playstation

. . . .
. . . .
. . . .
. . . .
. . . .
. . . .
. . . .
. . . . .Playstation.".

The game kicked off and it wasn't long before our English boys established their superiority. Thinking a few steps ahead of the opponent was the key – our players were clearly thinking as far ahead as next Saturday, such was their commitment and coordination. Across the nation, viewers were so entranced that in many cases they lost consciousness, such was the thrilling bill of footballing fare. The non-appearance of many spectators in the more prestigious seats, highlighted by TV cameras in the second half, can clearly be ascribed to their being detained en masse in the toilets, vomiting with tension. The key was tactical; the Swiss were up to their old trick of neutrality. Well, two can play at that game. And so, England, to a man, played too as if the whole business of attack, defence and aerial bombardment was just something that happened to other people.

Managerially, the England set-up has made a sound adjustment. The summary dismissal of Steve McClaren, upon discovery that he was a Scotchman, was a move in the right direction. I despised the Kylie Minogue-loving, coloured-umbrella-under-cowering, clueless, carrot-topped creep from the beginning and made no secret of my disdain. I do, however, greatly approve of the choice of replacement. It is a truth universally acknowledged that you could put a rusty, abandoned fridge in a blazer and appoint it manager of the England team, or even Bryan Robson, and it wouldn't make any difference, given the players at our disposal – we would still be England, with all the glory that entails. And so, much as Signor Mussolini was appointed Duce of Italy in order to add some light relief to what would otherwise have been in some ways a rather grim World War II, so the FA in their wisdom and indulgence appointed a random Italian, one Mr Capello, an illiterate barely capable of speaking. Naturally, he was "hhonorreed" to take the job – what bewildered, elderly Mediterranean peasant wouldn't be? - and so, he took his place in the dugout, with England's Mr Stuart Pearce on hand next to him, to explain what was going on during the game – the organ grinder, so to speak, to Mr Capello's monkey. It is right that the FA give Mr Capello their full support and backing – and perhaps a little fez.

Mr Pearce would have explained to Mr Capello that the fat man attempting to grow a beard charging around angrily like a rhinoceros with a malfunctioning tranquilliser dart hanging from his backside was England's finest footballing flower, Mr Wayne Rooney, engaged in a subtle process of attrition against the foe – and that that curious little fellow in the number 2 shirt at whom certain members of the crowd shouted "You know when you've been Tango'd" (a reference which, Seppings explains to me, appertains to the beverage of orangeade) every time he received the ball was Mr Wes Brown. Inevitably, English superiority, instilled by the expedient of long having realised that cheese is not a drink, told. Joe Cole pranced down the left wing like Tommy Trinder doing the Lambeth Walk and passed to Jenas, who slotted home. Doubtless, Mr Capello at this point would have leaned over to Stuart Pearce and remarked of the scorer, "Eeeeessss Eeenngland player, whhy eezz he ssoootface?" And Mr Pearce would have fielded the query with due tact and restraint.

Come the second half and England played on, as only England can. Switzerland scored a freak equaliser – had they dropped a bomb on Coventry in 1943 it would have been no more surprising. England, however, are made of stern spunk. Steven

Gerrard is such a warrior that even if he were passing a plate of sandwiches at a garden fête he would use a cannon in order to do so – his delivery was once again in that vein tonight. But his was a captain's performance. Peter Crouch could have added yet another goal, had he performed his trademark trick of assuming the shape of a swastika in order to meet the incoming cross. Why did he not? These were, after all, the Swiss - it is not as if they would have been offended.

TOMMY SUNDERLAND, NEWCASTLE UNITED SUPPORTER

The return of Kevin Keegan in January 2008 to beleaguered Newcastle United was a shot in the arm, but even His return could not prevent one or two heavy defeats early in his tenure. The ever-sanguine, if unfortunately nomen-clatured Tommy, however, is hopeful for the future and full of Toon faith.

Howay! Tommy Toon here. Well – Tommy Sunderland actually, but Newcastle through and through, Newcastle till I die, then I'd have to stop, like, on account of being dead. I've just seen the game against Villa – bit of a rollercoaster, that one. We were cock-a-hoop when trusty little Michael Owen nodded us one up and it looked like it was going to be our day. I don't know what "King" Kevin Keegan said to the lads at half time but it did them a power of good – even after they conceded a couple of quick goals at the beginning of the second half, they battled away just like you'd expect of a Keegan team, kept their heads up after Villa scored a third and showed typical "never say die" attitude when Villa popped in a fourth from the spot late on. You couldn't fault the Magpie spirit – it's just a shame they couldn't sneak those four goals that would have turned defeat into victory. Such a fine line. Still, like the man said, at the end of the day, that's football – as well as the rough, you have to take a few knocks.

One thing about Newcastle: players and managers may go on their travels, but the lure of St James is always liable to bring them back, the way it did Kevin, thank goodness, after he'd run away to join the circus and that. And why not? Newcastle's a grand town. We can offer some of the best Mars bars in the country and, to my mind, boast some of the most magnificent and eye-catching car parks in Great Britain also. It's like Paul "Gazza" Gascoigne – he went and found fame and fortune in the bright lights of London town, but I knew he'd return back north one day. And so he did, bonny lad. To Rangers, admittedly. But that didn't stop a whole crowd of us turning out to wave to him from the platform at Newcastle Station as his train passed through from London to Glasgow. A lot of us turned out again when he took the train from Glasgow to Middlesbrough, a few years later. I like to think he spotted us and waved back. There's always a pie, a Mars bar and a parking space awaiting him on Tyneside.

Gazza was one of the Toon legends all right. But like the man said, at the end of the day, he's not the only one. I think back over the last ten years, and some of the signings we've made – names like Steve Barton, Warren Taylor, Scott Taylor, Steve Warren, Taylor Parker, Scott Barton and Steve Parker. Between them, I'd reckon we paid a tidy £123 million for their services and great servants they've been to Newcastle United, especially in the relegation battles that followed them joining the club. Still, the daddy of them all, for my money, was Albert Shytehawke, centre forward of Newcastle's most recent league championship-winning team, in 1926-27. Young nippers today, you mention his name and they burst out laughing – it's understandable, I suppose, the name "Albert" sounds a bit quaint to kids in this day and age. But it's grand to hear a section of our support still honouring "Shyte"'s memory by chanting his nickname, as they have done quite a few times this season.

Anyway, I've got in my possession an old, yellowing cigarette card with a lovely pen and ink drawing of Albert Shytehawke, in his black knickerbockers standing on a laced football. It belonged to my grandfather, who'd had it passed down to him by his grandfather in turn. Sort of a family heirloom, really, even if it's got a bit stained over the years – nicotine, brown sauce and that. Anyway, that Antiques Roadshow came to town, so I thought I'd go down there and see what it might be worth, like. There was quite a queue, but I waited me turn and eventually I'm in front of one of their experts, feller with a moustache, who looks up, a bit testy.

"Well?" he says. So I pull out me cigarette card. He looks at it as if he doesn't even recognise Albert Shytehawke.

"What the fuck's this?" he says, which took me aback, because you don't expect that sort of talk off telly . "Have you been wiping your arse with it, or what?"

"It's a family heirloom, like," I explained. "Collector's item, I should think. Albert Shytehawke. Big hero round these parts. Scored 56 goals in 1926-27. Not sure if they had goalkeepers back then, but – anyway, I was just wondering what it might be worth."

He tosses it back at me. "I'd give you a quid."

"A pound?"

"Yeah. A pound." And he fished one out of his pocket. "You fucking people. Talk about timewasters – I just had a bloke show me a shoe. One shoe. He said he'd lost the other one. Here you are, there's a pound. I'm paying you a pound to go away, basically, not for this piece of arsewipe. Get it? It's a "Fuck off" pound."

Well, you can imagine what I made of that. A pound's a lot of money and I admit I was tempted. But in the end, I decided the card was of too strong sentimental value so I thanked him for his kind offer but declined, and took my leave. Like the man said, at the end of the day, you can't put a price on some things.

I always watch Toon games at the Shinner's Arms. Funny, really, because me and the landlord don't always see eye to eye. It's one thing that you can't smoke tabs in the pub any more, but now he's introduced a new "no farting" rule as well. Said there'd been complaints, about me in particular. Farting's one of the few pleasures I have in life and I've always farted considerately but without the smoke to mask the smell, well, there's your problem in a nutshell. So now I have to go outside to break wind, which at this time of year, well, it's cold, when all you're wearing is a string vest. But like the man said, at the end of the day, that's progress.

Thing about the Shinner's Arms is, it's my lucky pub. I was here a few seasons ago, when Newcastle played Chester in the FA Cup 3rd round, at home. I was so proud of our lads that day. If pride, passion, commitment and effort counted for anything on the scoreboard, we would have run out 10-0 victors. As it was, we went down 0-2, a result which flattered Chester, to my mind. Anyway, I was drowning my sorrows, feeling a bit down in the dumps afterwards and I mumbled to the landlord, "I must admit, Len, I was expecting better from our lads than that."

"What's that?" I turn round and there's this lad, a Chester supporter I could tell by his scarf, in a smart grey suit. Some sort of salesman, I think. Cut above, drank his beer out of a bottle.

"What's that?" he repeats.

"Well, I was just saying - "

"Yeah, I know what you were saying. Typical fucking Premiership aristocrat attitude. You sit up there on your perch and think you've a divine fucking right to win against the little teams like us! You were all high and mighty, you thought all you needed to do was turn up, take a giant dump on us! Well, just for once, just for once, it was the underdogs' turn. Yeah, yeah, we

haven't got money to throw around like you spoilt arseholes..."
as he said this, he produced a wad of £20 notes with a silver clip
and started waving it around. "Think you can laugh at us for
being dirt poor? Well, we may not have your money, but we've
got something you Premiership glory-hunters forgot about years
ago. We've got integrity. We've got soul. And every now and
then, you fat cats get complacent and we turn you over. So take
your spanking, you with your big stadium and executive boxes.
You've no idea what it's like in the lower leagues, losing, week in,
week out. Well, you've had a taste of it now, you! You make me
puke my fucking ring, you arrogant, self-righteous scumbags!"
And with that, he sups up his bottle, storms out the pub, climbs
in his BMW and drives off. Well, the last laugh was on him, like,
because if he'd known, just 100 yards down the road, there's one
of the most splendid car parks in all of the North East – ten
storeys high. It was opened in 2003, after they knocked down the
old community centre. Sometimes, if I fancy treating myself, I
like to go down to that car park, you know, just to look around.

Anyway, I had hoped to watch the Villa game at the Shinners,
but I'm actually writing this from hospital. See, I had a bit of a
run-in last night. I'd been saving my brown coins all year for one
of them customised club football shirts – y'know, the ones with
your name on the back. Well, it came back yesterday. So I decided
to give the string vest the night off and wore it down the pub. I'd
hardly walked in the door, when one of this group of lads, our
lads y'know, Toon, taps me on the shoulder.

"What the fook's this, like? What's with the shirt? Some sort of
joke, or what? You tanna piss? 'Sunderland'?"

"Yes!" I said. "See, that's me. I'm Sunderland."

"You're Sunderland?"

"Aye. Sunderland. That's me."

Well, you know, sometimes there's no explaining things to
these big lads and the top and bottom of it is, I was in overnight
for minor concussion and two broken ribs. I tell you, if Newcastle

United can demonstrate the same passion, strength and commitment to the task these lads displayed as they beat the daylights out of me, then we've nothing to fear this season. Toon!

In February 2008, Liverpool Football Club were knocked out of the FA Cup by lowly Barnsley. A nation shared their grief, as SELF RIGHTEOUS LIVERPOOL FAN soberly recounts.

IT'S NOT WHAT LIVERPOOL DO AGAINST BARNSLEY, IT'S WHAT'S IN OUR GUTS AND HEARTS

An eerie paralysis has settled like a fog across the city of Liverpool this morning. Bicycles, upon which kids performed wheelies around shopping malls just yesterday morning, lie abandoned. No whistled melody plays on the lips of the milkman as he does his rounds. Jimmy Tarbuck and Tom O' Connor, for once in their lives, have only completely unfunny observations to make. At TV rental shop windows, hushed folk gather around in the hope of updates on our manager, who surely faces a fight for his life over the next several days. At Anfield, fans form a long, patient queue, waiting to sign a Book of Condolence and leave floral tributes at the point where the tragedy occurred, just 25 yards from the hallowed Kop End. One, spelled out in red and white roses, reads simply "BARNSLEY??" This is a city united in grief, under the world spotlight, a city wondering to itself; did John Lennon of The Beatles die for this? George Harrison? Stuart Sutcliffe?

This is a time for mourning, and for lessons to be learned from the dreadful events of what will be known as 16/2. And the first lesson that needs to be learned is by the friggin' Barnsley players, in how to read. In case they didn't notice, there's a sign above your heads as you come out of the dressing room that reads "THIS IS ANFIELD". It's supposed to put the fear of Yosser Hughes into you. You don't ignore that sign, you quail and genuflect. Then you go out and lie down as Liverpool Football Club walk tall, with passion and pride in their hearts and guts in their bellies, all over you.

It was quite obvious the way Barnsley played that they had completely the wrong attitude. No respect for their betters, or for the sacred turf they charged around on like kids misbehaving in church. How can you play like that, desecrating the memory of great players like Tommy Lawrence, Tommy Smith, Emlyn Hughes and Jimmy Carter with every last-ditch clearance, slide tackle and friggin' 25-yard screamer? How can you do that in front of the Kop, where surging fans would sing Gerry & The Pacemakers songs and piss in each other's pockets? That was the community spirit we had back then – every man a toilet for his neighbour. There were no inside lavs back in the 60s, remember – when you needed to go, you knocked on the door of feller in the next house along, he'd let you in, and you'd go in his overcoat pocket. And you'd do the same for him. Great days. Talk of the "romance of the Cup" rings sick and hollow this morning. To people who say that, I say – Myra Hindley and Ian Brady. Was that romantic? It was not. Neither was this. Cilla Black has quite literally been laid prostrate and defecated upon from a height of 30 metres once more, then forced to crawl around eating the plop that didn't land directly in her mouth. Cilla. Our Cilla. Well, I hope you're happy.

But we are Liverpool. Over the next few days, the watching world will see an example of how a city copes with adversity, its citizens united, never walking alone, standing together, showing solidarity in their grief, except for the Everton scum, the city of Liverpool, together in unison as one.

There is a time for grieving but also a time for bitter recrimination. So, as of this morning, I am organising a city-wide boycott of all Barnsley products. Coal. Clogs. Michael Parkinson autobiographies. Barnsley shall feel the wrath of the people of Liverpool where it hurts. I'm also organising a Barnsley Appeal Fund. I'm hoping Margi Clark will agree to sing a few songs at a big show I'm planning, maybe get Paul McCartney to write one of them oratorios of his, in honour and memory of the Heroes who Fell At the Fifth, or reunite the cast of Bread to record a rousing version of "You'll Never Walk Alone". 'Cos, you see, I've realised, if there's one thing we can learn from the tragedy that was 16/2, it's that we, Liverpool Football Club, need to buy more players. Stevie, Jamie, Stevie, they're great la's but they can't do it all by themselves. Maybe, in future, a tragedy like this could be averted if we threw more money at a bunch of players who turned out to be un-useless and totally succeeded in gelling. That, and appoint Ricky Tomlinson as team manager. Passion! Heart! . . .

ENGLAND V FRANCE (Friendly)
March 26, 2008

The increasingly strikingly bearded Nicolas Anelka is brought down by David James - Franck Ribery converts the spot kick. David Beckham celebrates his 100th cap. Rio Ferdinand, perhaps due to his characteristic powers of concentration, is appointed captain.

EXCELLENT ENGLISHMEN ROUT CRYING FRENCHWOMEN 0-1

In 1956, in the United Kingdom, the first Clean Air Act was introduced. The Act was passed by common consent and welcomed by Britons as a milestone in the history of this sceptr'd isle. Cities became smoke- and soot-free zones, and the Lord God Almighty was able to look fondly down from Heaven upon his most favoured nation, his view unimpeded by smog. A few years later, by contrast, across the unmercifully narrow channel in France, there was an attempt to pass the Clean Armpit Act. This was designed to bring the French nation into line with the rest of Europe in matters of personal sanitation and hygiene, and generally to maintain the proper disparity between man and chimpanzee. From Lille in the north, however, to Marseilles in the south, there was a national outcry at the proposal. Town halls were occupied, boulevards blocked by sit-in protesters brandishing placards, bathtubs smashed with sledgehammers in the streets and a general strike declared. Notably, the nation's women were among the most vociferous of the demonstrators, very much to the fore at the barricades, ranting, raving and reeking. When the authorities threatened to send in the army, the response of the rebelling populace was not one of trepidation but ribald amusement - as if, as one eminent historian commented, the government had threatened to send in the homosexuals. Eventually, efforts to pass the Clean Armpit Act were abandoned and the French festered triumphantly once more in a collective miasma of their own body odour.

That there is a small element of fabrication in the above story – it was composed by myself in the early 1970s as part of a pamphlet extolling the virtues of keeping Britain well out of the Common Market and all its horrors – is no matter. Indeed, though I made the whole thing up, it rings entirely true to me today. For it speaks a deeper truth about the rankness of our foes upon the field of play tonight. Let us consider the matter. In recent years, Great Britain has, with in certain cases the token assistance of our former colonial subjugates the United States, won a notable series of wars. Among our conquests are Sierre Leone, Iraq, Yugoslavia, Afghanistan and Argentina. Whom have the French gone to war against in the meantime? Greenpeace. And, thanks to the intervention of the mighty New Zealand, they lost. Bested, by an enemy who marched in edible sandals. Moreover, ruminate upon the following, cogitate upon the contrasts. Here is a nation whose most famous sons – Jacques Brel, Tin Tin, Monsieur Poirot, Maigret – turn out, upon closer inspection, to be Belgian. In England, to suggest that one eats a piece of cake is considered the epitome of good manners, not grounds for summary decapitation. In England, our greatest thinkers and philosophers – Newton, Kipling, Powell – have tackled the basic questions, such as gravity, why the English are the proper bearers of the white man's burden, and the racial question. In France, what do their "thinkers" fret upon? "Being". Yes, while John Bull can quite happily "be" all day long without effort - after all, it's not that ruddy difficult - for the French, it seems, merely to exist is as onerous to them as maintaining the Maginot line. Which makes it all the more ironic that Frenchmen manage to "be" two things at once – that is to say, excessively heterosexual and ragingly homosexual at the same time.

To look upon the respective maps of the two nations is instructive. First, the British Isles. There She sits, with a head-like shape, plume resplendent, shapely and recumbent, with Anglia as an uplifted backside, breaking wind in the general direction of continental Europe. As for the French nation, well, let us conduct a scientific experiment. Let us emulate the national pastime of our Gallic neighbours, unbutton our flies and relieve ourselves openly on the pavement.

The resultant splash will, in all probability, form the shape of France. For that is what France is – a urine stain upon Europe. The matter is scientifically proven.

The national anthems, as ever, exposed the great contrast between our two absurdly closely situated nations. Our own is conducted at the measured pace of a slow advance across the battlefield, bayonets raised. By contrast, the French anthem is played, not inappropriately, at the pace of a brisk retreat. Our anthem stresses our desire to save our Queen – the French, for their part, are constitutionally preoccupied with concealing their mistresses. Queens versus mistresses – that was what was at stake in this fixture.

The match began at a cautious pace – one was absorbingly reminded of the opening 15 minutes of the Hundred Years War. Midway through the first half, the score was not nil-nil but, more strictly speaking, nil-Nothingness – which made us effectively in the lead. The key to Steven Gerrard's career success has been that he has always aimed high – and so he did, several times in the first half. To paraphrase the female in the motion flicker picture Sunset Boulevard, it was not any failing on Gerrard's part – it was the goalposts that got small. Absurdly, the Al-Qaeda member in France's midst made a shock attack upon England's sovereign territory and, rather then being dispatched forthwith to Guantanamo Bay, was awarded a penalty – such is French treachery in the face of Islamist outrage.

Come the second half and England continued to advance, showing their innate superiority. This has always been evident – one notes in recent years the onfield, foppish jinks of Messrs Henry and Cantona who, week in week out, proved themselves singularly unable to conform to the demands of the English game. ("Pressure! Harry! Honesty! Give it! Hoof! Anywhere will do!") That one Englishman is worth eight Frenchmen is all too evident when one considers our coffee consumption. A Frenchman can evidently only take a thimbleful of coffee at a time, whereas we English can consume a half pint mug of the instant variety without a qualm. It would take eight Frenchman to drink a single English mug of coffee. Hence, our overwhelming dominance in the opposing penalty box. One move stands out in particular – between the frighteningly effective Stewart Downing and the England number 3, whom, I understand from Seppings' notes, is affectionately known to one and all as "Twatley Cunt". In the interests of jovial camaraderie, I shall address him thus. So went the move. "Cunt. To Downing. Back to Cunt. Cunt lingers. Cunt passes back to Downing. Downing back to Cunt. Cunt. Cunt!! Cunt!!! Shoot, Cunt!! Oh you, Cunt!"

Michael Owen showed great promise once more – once he has grown a little, perhaps to the same height as his colleague Peter Crouch, he will undoubtedly fulfil his potential. "Square headed,

Britney Spears-type busted flush" is what he indubitably is not.

A word concerning the appointment of Rio Ferdinand as England captain. As I have mentioned before, the FA amusingly saw fit to appoint an illiterate Italian imbecile as England manager, if only to point out how superfluous and ceremonial the role is, and rightly so. One might surmise that he had emulated his ancient countryman Caligula, who appointed a horse as a senator. More probably, Stuart Pearce and the rest of his superiors in the English set-up doubtless blindfolded the confused old peasant and turned him about in a game of "pin the tail on the donkey" when making the appointment. Certainly, Ferdinand lived up well to his responsibilities – his thought processes were clear throughout the match. "Ball goes up . . . . ball goes down . . . . ball goes up . . . . ball goes down . . . . ball goes up . . . . ball goes down . . . . ball goes up . . . . ball goes down . . . . ball goes up . . . . ball goes down . . . . ball goes up . . . . ball goes down . . . . Playstation . . . ball goes up . . . . ball goes down . . . .".

However, it would have been still more prudent had the FA appointed our warlike Prince Harry as England captain, bringing back memories of Agincourt, the sacking of Harfleur and the routing of the Gallic popinjays on their own muddy fields. English players a-bed like Michael Carrick would have held their manhoods cheap that they were not beside him on the field of play, but that would doubtless have stiffened their sinews for the next fixture.

But let us return to this matter of the Clean Armpit Act. I propose that England's finest and most fragrant flower, John Terry, be sent on an ambassadorial mission across the length and breadth of France to instruct citizens and peasantry alike in the rudiments of proper bathing, wheeled by mobile bathtub to and from every city, every village, every hamlet. I would happily accompany Mr Terry on the mission, armed with my faithful loofah and flannel, and demonstrate upon his person the most effective techniques of all-over body-washing. My ability to communicate effectively with the French – that is, bellow slowly and repeatedly in plain English – would stand me in excellent stead. In front of small, gathered crowds, I would have Mr Terry disrobe, then step into the bathtub. There, with running commentary, I would apply soap to his chest and stomach, working up an impressive foam in the process. We'll make Englishmen of these Frenchwomen yet . . .

ENGLAND V USA (Friendly)
MAY 28, 2008

John Terry sets aside the tears and disappointment of his unamusingly ill-directed penalty kick in the Champions League final days earlier, leading England to victory over a lacklustre American team.

EXEMPLARY ENGLAND'S GOLDEN GENERATION SHOWER USA 2-0

In 1944, as a senior officer in the Covert British Operations Unit, I witnessed from my seaborne position to the rear the D-Day invasion of Omaha Beach by American troops, as they sought to loosen the Nazi grip on the European mainland. I saw as these helmeted "GIs" waded ashore, in wave after wave, many of them drowning, many of them mown down by German troops stationed in nests overlooking the beach, still many more of them succumbing to bullets dispatched by myself from my trusty revolver. For, although the Americans were technically on the British side, the more farsighted among us anticipated the deleterious influence these jazz-crazed, swaggering hat-cockers were likely to have upon civilisation if not discreetly culled whenever possible during the great conflicts. These, you must understand, were the sort of people who complained if chewing gum were not featured on the menus in restaurants, the sort of people who were as incapable of pronouncing the letter "t" as they were of comprehending the chortlesome quips of "Big Hearted" Arthur Askey, the sort of people whose golf-ball-sized brains were unable to make sense of the word "plough" and, like the superfatted infants they were, decreed that it be spelt "plow". No doubt, by their logic, the word "cough" should be spelt "cow", to avoid confusion. Coughs versus cows. That was what was at stake in this vital fixture tonight.

Vital indeed it was, the most important England game to have taken place since 1776, when our former colonial subjugates achieved a temporary state of independence. We have been biding our time since then. This was the clash of the world's Big Two, both significant players at the Yalta Summit in 1945, which saw the post-war world sensibly carved up by British civil servants using their pencils and set squares, to subsequent, harmonious effect. And, like Yalta, it reduces the forthcoming Euro 2008 convention of our European cousins to a mere trifle by comparison.

The national anthems indicated the contrast between the two teams, the two nations. The British rendition was delivered manfully, without frills, braying out the hope that our cherished Elizabeth be saved as surely as an innocuous Croatian long-distance shot by Scott Carson. The American anthem, meanwhile, performed by a negress, was not so much sung as very slowly vomited, as if regurgitating a typical American breakfast of waffles, molasses, honey, blueberry jam, whipped cream and treacle. The USA team clasped their hands to their heart and sang along lustily, with pitch microphones picking up goalkeeper Timothy Howard's contributions; "Land of the . . . COCKFERRETS!! . . .and the home of the . . . CUNTBUBBLE-FARTERS!!" (Ah, Monsieur Tourette, you may have invented the syndrome, but it was we Anglo-Saxons who took the ball and ran with it.)

It is, of course, inherently absurd that the USA should be playing their masters England at the game of association football, and it was the job of the referee and his assistants to go around to each American player and confiscate from them any helmets, padding or bats they might have imported onto the field of play in their burger-brained imbecility, as well as to explain to them that the game would not cease every two minutes to provide for ten-minute breaks for advertisements for dog shampoo. The game was conducted at a brisk pelt, with England providing a masterclass in how almost to string two passes together without the ball bouncing loose for a fucking throw-in to the opposition. The Americans provided no worries – it was anticipated that, in keeping with their war record, they would not themselves actually participate in the game until midway through the second half. "Manager" Fabio Capello, hired as an amusing joke to show that even a witless Euro-Simean could be nominally put in charge of the England team, prudently did not object when his bowler-hatted English masters decreed that young prospects David Beckham and Jermain Defoe be given the chance to show what they are made of, and what they might contribute to the team when they hit their stride and their early forties.

There were other notable performances. Wes Brown, who owns two European Cup medals, showed how and why he is twice the player Bobby Charlton is, who owns but one. Frank Lampard paid a touching tribute to his late mother by playing as if he himself no longer existed, while Wayne Rooney showed the doubters that he is, indeed, England's angriest, hairiest, most frustrated potato. But it was John Terry, reborn again, purged in adversity yet emerging a stronger, handsomer man for his experiences, who truly inspired, and even changed the mindset of some of us. It has always been my belief that only homosexual men cry. However, having seen John Terry's display I am now of the firm conviction that "trick photography" is more advanced than many of us anticipated – and that a conspiracy is afoot among television companies to besmirch the masculinity of our great captain.

As New Yorkers mass nervously in Times Square, looking anxiously at the ticker-tape reading "0-2 . . . ALL IS LOST, ALL IS LOST", it is clear that America's assumption of independence from the Empire has been conclusively discredited. It is high time that the British ambassador present his compliments to the incumbent Mr George Bush and insist that governorship of the United States be handed over to a British Royal – Prince Edward, perhaps, who could juggle the role of American overseer with the running of his small theatre company. Either that or face the wrath of his military brother, Prince Andrew. Once more unto the beach, dear friends . . .

ENGLAND V TRINIDAD & TOBAGO (Friendly)
June 1, 2008

Jermain Defoe knocks in a couple as England once more test their mettle against familiar Caribbean opposition. There are suggestions that the fixture only went ahead to curry favour with Jack Warner, controversial head of the Trinidad & Tobago Football Federation and FIFA vice-President.

INESTIMABLE ENGLAND THRASH INFERIOR CARIBBEANS 3-0

In a match which all observers, whether patriotic or treacherous, agree was the finest of the 2006 World Cup, England bested tonight's opponents 2-0, following a contest as tense and hard-fought as Rorke's Drift – in this case, Yorke's drift. Plucky little England eventually broke the deadlock thanks to plucky little Peter Crouch, who scored by the expedient of clambering all over the back of a black man to his winning advantage. Some cried "unfair" - effeminate polytechnic lecturers and adenoidal social workers in the main – but the larger-minded among us applauded Mr Crouch for reaffirming the basis of our civilisation. Had we not clambered all over the backs of black men two centuries ago, we would not have established the great plantations which are the cornerstone of this sceptr'd isle's wealth, enabling us to lead the world as purveyors of, among other things, fair play and spotted dick. The referee did not intervene against Crouch in 2006; nor did the referee of world affairs, the Lord God Almighty Himself, back in the 18th century.

I did not anticipate that we would have to re-engage in this Homeric struggle; however, since 2006, there has been a dark, Conradian twist of fate. Jack Warner, who once entertained the British nation as the kindly Sergeant in Dixon Of Dock Green, visited the Caribbean on some pretext or other and evidently went native, setting up his own, sinister federation, CONCACAF, whose headquarters are doubtless in some submarine aquadome guarded by boiler-suited henchmen, from where he plots Trinidadian and Tobagan global domination, with his demented self at the helm. As England showed in their fixture against the Americans, a Bond is always far more use than a Felix Leiter in these situations – and so, it came down once more to England to fight out what was not just the most important fixture of the season but, in its symbolism, arguably the most important association football match played since World War II. This was about a clash of antithetical lifestyles; working 60 hours a week and holidaying on rainy caravan sites or working 60 hours a year and mostly idling under coconut trees drinking green cocktails. We knew which one had to prevail. Of course, it was Trinidad and Tobago, two against one – it could only be hoped that England could emulate the feat of unfancied Manchester United, who against the odds beat both Brighton and Hove Albion to win the Football Association Challenge Cup in 1983.

The national anthems saw the unruly, indigenous team throw down the first insult, epitomising their archipelagic awfulness. They played our own, sacred anthem on what appeared to be battered dustbin lids. Had a mob of their men held our Queen at spearpoint and forcibly inserted bananas in her orifices, they could not have offered a more grotesque slight. This fired up our men. Steven Gerrard played like a man possessed, if not always of the ball, though this was of no matter to those who value patriotism and pride over actually playing with a bit of fucking intelligence and not like some bloodbrained, remedially haircutted twathead. The decision made by Fabio Capello's handlers, of which they informed him upon letting him out of the crate in which he travelled to the Caribbean, to make David Beckham captain was laudable and farsighted – the decision not to emphasise his imperial carriage by having him play in a plumed hat was, to my mind, less so. Gareth Barry had about him the composed air of a plantation owner's son who would brook no insubordination from the fields, and he it was who struck the first blow against Trinidadian and Tobagan insolence with the opening goal. There, the matter ought to have ended, with the match abandoned and the Trinidadian and Tobagan players each fined 90 minutes' wages for being away from their workplaces. However, they had the temerity to rally. These were not the smiling, grinning Caribbean types of our youths and marmalade jars. It is notable that they played Stern John, rather than Happy Joe (such are the nomenclatures of these fellows). Still, when our own Jermain Defoe (for whom an apology to his fellow English players for the behaviour of his Caribbean kind was doubtless forthcoming after the match) scored twice, the matter was as good as settled. He could even afford to spurn a third, instead aiming the ball high over the bar, presenting it as a gift to the grateful people of Venezuela.

Victory was absolutely vital to secure. Had Trinidad and Tobago somehow won this day, the scenes in such negro strongholds as Notting Hill would have been too much to bear – there would have been gloating, inevitably breeding, and, within a generation, following a demographic shift to their advantage, compulsory limbo dancing in the British Isles. This would not stand, not in Dorset, not in Totteridge. Now, let us press home our advantage. Let us break the Caribbean hold on Notting Hill. Let the bravest of our white citizens, who hold the future of the race at heart, move into this benighted area of West London and establish enclaves there. Perhaps our filmmakers could even make strategically insipid motion pictures, depicting the area as an exclusively white district, a serene backdrop for the romantic caperings of stammering Englishmen.

As for John Terry's absence, I understand the FA's wisdom in this matter. He may not yet be sound. They saw what happened when Jack Warner travelled upriver to Trinidad. Could the same not happen to John Terry, his fine mind turned in those sweltering climes? One imagines him going AWOL, establishing some mountain stronghold, head shaved, sitting in a makeshift throne, surrounded by the skulls of Trinidadians on poles, worshipped by the locals, rocking back and forth murmuring quietly to himself, "Must forget Moscow! Must forget Moscow!" as natives dance around him chanting in unison, "Must forget Moscow! Must forget Moscow!" There he sits, the veins in his temple throbbing, his near-naked torso glowing with sweat beads, in his mind, slipping over and re-enacting that fateful miss and murmuring to himself, "The horror." (Action replay) "The horror."

ENGLAND V CZECH REPUBLIC (Friendly)
August 20, 2008

With Great Britain having taken an impressive haul of medals at the Olympics, an anxious nation awaits to see if the England football team can keep their end up. Sadly, this is an uncharacteristically lacklustre performance, with uncharacteristically lukewarm application from some of the bigger names.

EXEMPLARY ENGLAND BALANCE BAD CZECHS 2-2

During this miserable Olympiad, in which, by perfidious means one can only speculate upon, foreigners have dominated the medals haul (Romero, Houvenaghel, Ohuruogu and, sticking like a thistle in the craw, the Scotchman Hoy), it has fallen to England's mighty footballing XI to restore the pride in British sports that is our manifest due. This match is without doubt the most important to have taken place at Wembley in many years. It was both inevitable and vital that we see off the sallow Czechs, a nation who subsist on vegetables British horses would refuse if they were mixed into their nosebags. Lose this match, and such would be the national humiliation, we might as well go the whole hog and make Fabio Capello, presently our amusing Italian mascot, team manager, with Manuel, he of the British Broadcasting Corporation's situation comedy, his assistant. Here is a nation so perversely devoted to its own chronic historical and cultural misery that they put accents on their consonants, the linguistic equivalent of insisting that all citizens bash themselves repeatedly on the heads with iron frying pans before setting out to work. Here is a nation so woefully shorthanded that for a while their playwright had to double up as their President.

The national anthems, as ever, spelt out the true story. Our own bespeaks lofty and ambitious sentiments - murder the Scots, enable our dear Queen to live to the age of 203, and so forth. As for the Czech effort, its sentiments could be paraphrased thus: "Towards a colour television set in every town by the year 2050." It seems that post-war Czech history was in part determined by their resentment of the fact that whereas when Germany invaded Poland in 1939, Britain declared the commencement of World War II, when Germany invaded Czechoslovakia in 1938, Britain wasn't overly bothered, sending over Mr Neville Chamberlain in a small plane from Croydon airport clutching a peace pact. The Czechs took offence but perhaps they should have taken stock -

reviewing, perhaps, how Great Britain's strategic decisions reflected upon the Czechs' manners, morals, deportment, physical complexion and smell.

Certainly, there was something about the way the Czech team hungrily regarded the ball in the opening 20 or so minutes of this fixture which prompted one to suspect that they imagined it to be some form of especially delicious dumpling, unknown to their own cuisine. It was gallant indeed of England's players, conscious of their responsibilities as hosts towards their guests, to give the ball to them time and again, in order that they might muster some simian effort on goal, restoring their pride as humans-in-waiting. However, as the game progressed, it became clear that there was a gulf in standards between the two teams. The Czechs reminded of the Axis, abject and defeated of Europe - the Dutch, the Germans, the Italians, the Spanish. By contrast, England's football could be summarised in two words: First Division.

David Beckham was sagely given the full 90 minutes to show what this young player might potentially have to offer England in the coming years, particularly if the footballing laws were relaxed and he were allowed to bring his caddy onto the field for key set pieces. ("Number six boot, please.") However, it speaks volumes that if his wife, Victoria, had been partnering him in midfield, England could have performed no fucking worse. By the same token, Milan Baros was playing upfront for the Czechs. However, had Milan Kundera been playing in his place, England would probably have fared no fucking better, such was the extent of their dominance of this game. It was Baros however who, beggaring all expectation, opened the scoring for the foreigners, by insidious dint of resorting to the tactics of the animal kingdom. The way he jutted out his backside when turning our beloved captain and inspiration John Terry was a clear example of "presenting", one which would have shocked our Big Personality to his ardently heterosexual core.

Particularly galling was the brazen way in which our opponents took advantage of lax and fluid border control among the less ruly Eastern European nations. That the Czech goalkeeper went by the name of Cech was all well and good; however, that they also fielded a player by the name of "Polak" suggested an underhand cross-border cooperation alien to our own Corinthian Code. Who else might have been waiting in the wings had substitutions permitted? "Russki"? "Kraut"? Of course, we had our own "Brown", though his surname is more in the nature of a confession. He it was, however, whose head connected unwittingly with a David Beckham corner kick to even the score.

Of the free kick with which the Czechs further advanced their tally in the second half we shall not dwell. It was clear to one and all that England were not ready for the set piece - indeed will not be for about another 40 years. David James, the goalkeeper, is not to be blamed. It may well be that following a botched appointment at the hairdressers, he was forced to improvise his coiffure with the assistance of a marker pen. However, this makes him much the superior of his opposite number Cech, whose headjoy made him look like a member of some peripatetic troupe of sex educationalists, with himself starring in the role of "Mr Prophylactic".

Let us dwell, rather, upon the countless positives for our young lions. If the Caribbean gentleman Usain Bolt has appeared somewhat euphoric this past week or so, it is in the knowledge that he has not had to contend with the fearsome turn of pace of David Beckham in Beijing. Emile Heskey and Jermaine Jenas's selection suggests that England's new young crop of talent are improving with each passing decade. As for Frank Lampard, well, there may well be Richard Dawkins-type sceptics who wonder whether he exists at all and, if he does, why he never makes any sort of significant intervention. Well, those of us who have faith that he does exist were vindicated when he manifested himself late in the second half, trotting off for a late substitution.

Finally, England attained the final, and deciding, goal with an elaborately worked manoeuvre which suggests a good deal of premeditation on the training ground - and proves, as does tonight's performance as a whole, that these players know each other inside out, as opposed to what they read about each other in the tabloids.

If I might venture a constructive suggestion on a night of such flawlessness, it is that our mascot, Mr Capello, is being insufficiently well used to best effect merely sitting in the dugout in a suit. Since he, or his Italian impresario master, are being paid for, they should be made to work for their fee. I suggest that Capello take to the field next time in a hal- time entertainment special, wearing a hooped jersey, shouting "Mamma Mia!" and suchlike, eventually falling full in the face into a pan of spaghetti he is carrying, perhaps being speared in the backside by a disgruntled Abyssinian whose country he has attempted to invade for good measure as he retreats the pitch.

And finally, a small quibble - given John Terry's preferment as captain, the biggest news story of 2008, he should have been greeted onto the pitch by his fellow players with what one might euphemistically describe as a 21 gun salute. Each man on each team administered with rifles, and, so as not to insult our captain's mettle, neither fired harmlessly into the air nor loaded with blanks. Live bullets, sir. He has the skull and the torso of an Englishman to withstand them, along with all foreign brickbats.

In March 2008, Liverpool came to the Emirates and knocked Arsenal out of the Champions League in the Quarter finals. HARTLEY SEBAG-FFIENNES, ARSENAL SUPPORTER and SELF-RIGHTEOUS LIVERPOOL FAN went head to head in their reminiscences.

HARTLEY: "Base, base, all is base/Cry sooth, the goodly Childe is thwarted at the tourney by the coarse Coxcomb/And the angels do weep salt tears in lachrymose rage at the marble hearted foulness of Prince Providence".

My own words, penned in the style of the Bard but possessing, of course, a certain felicitous refinement of which Shakespeare himself, not being London-born and hidebound by the iambic meter, was incapable. These were the words I bellowed upon the final whistle's blast, and my fellow Arsenal fans nodded, before taking up the chant themselves. A trilogy has drawn to a close, one which has turned out to be Euripidian in its tragic outcome. Mute is the songbird upon its perch, silent the swan upon the lake of lamentation. Of course, the very fact that this troglodyte rabble, this Liverpool Football Club, won the Champions League in 2005, gives pause – not unlike turning up at the Civic Hall annual ball and finding one's master butcher in attendance, one feels the entire event is cheapened altogether. Dirk Kuyt; does his countenance not have the unmistakable air of a cow's backside following repeated battery with a banjolele? How can our players, men of the most exquisite sensibility, be expected to mark a cow-man from whom they are compelled to avert their eyes in disgust?

SELF-RIGHTEOUS: They say there's only two teams in Liverpool – the one Rafa Benitez picks one week, then the one he picks the next. Well, this was the one he picked last night, and we walked tall in the shirt. There's been some memorable nights in Anfield, especially in the 90s – there was Racing Boys of Berne in 1996 (0-0), FC Lederhosen, 1997 (0-0), St. Ponce, 1998 (0-0), matches which brought the blood rushing to the acne on your forehead, pulsating results which summoned up all the passion you think of when you hear the words "Liverpool, Wednesday, November." But this was special, this. This was a night that made you realise just how much Liverpool is Liverpool and how much everywhere that isn't Liverpool isn't, how much Steven Gerrard is Steven Gerrard and how much you down south aren't. "Liverpool, Liverpool, we walk tall/You are not, so you walk small."

HARTLEY: It was the invidious task of the stalwart staff of the Emirates stadium to play host not once but twice to the barely sentient fans of "Liverpool FC" ("Faecal Crust"?) once they had wended their way, in some base parody of the Jarrow March, to London. To watch them set foot in our beloved cathedral one felt like the curator looking on in horror as swine were herded through the National Gallery. I myself felt the anguish keenly as, in my capacity as Senior Corporate Interior Design Consultant, I had a hand in some of the finer details of the construction of the Arsenal stadium. It piqued me no little, therefore, when I heard reports of the behaviour of some Liverpool fans upon completion of the game last Wednesday. With Arsenal stewards urging them, as politely as is appropriate, with bullhorns and wolfhounds, to take their leave, it seems that a great many of them did not comply but rather tarried. These malodorous refuseniks later complained that they could not find their way out of the stadium. What balderdash. At the away end, at my specification, there is a sign clearly marked "EGRESS". What can you do with such barnyard dwellers?

SELF-RIGHTEOUS: I remember me first trip down to London, me, on the Wally Arnold in 1987 to see them play Arsenal in that Milk Cola Final. As we were going down towards Wembley Way, there were these Arsenal fans, right, waving little bunches of paper at us with the numbers "5" and "10" on them. We all turned to each other and said, what the frig's all that about? It was only a couple of years later when I saw Degsy Hatton in WH Smiths hand over one of them that I knew this was London money. Well, I'm telling you, after tonight's performance, I reckon Jamie Carragher deserves to be awarded one of those bits of number ten London paper – and if it were up to me, he'd get one every year of his life till the day he dies, a Red through and through. We look after our own. Other players tackle. Not good enough. Not good enough for Liverpool Football Club. Jamie TAAACCCCHHHHKKKLLLEEES. He slides on his backside through his own saliva to save the day. For Cilla. For Margi. For Carla. For Liverpool Football Club. We wear the shirt.

HARTLEY: Before the commencement of the game, a Liverpudlian official – the man the city sent out of the town to university, presumably – bade us observe a silence. Decency, compassion and the Corinthian way being our hallmarks, we Arsenal fans duly did so, for the duration of the game. It disgusts me to report that the silence was frequently interrupted throughout the match, however, by the Liverpool contingent, who maintained a constant drone of base lowing and a urinal shower of verbal derision. The Arsenal team are noted by their manager and moral mentor M. Wenger on a weekly basis for their "resilience". This, they possess. They ask only for their performances to be greeted with the sort of deference one would expect at Crufts when a high pedigree poodle is trotted out to compete for the rosette of Best In Show. Even this rudimentary level of respect is lacking among the "Scousers" (why are their self-created nomenclatures almost deliberately designed to be such that one must wipe oneself down with a chamois leather when they utter them at you?). The contrast of styles was marked from the outset. Arsenal's play was like some advanced, exquisite form of calligraphy, Liverpool's the equivalent of a pig scratching out a mark in which to defecate in the dirt. Whenever Liverpool put the ball in the box, it was with the finesse of a Liverpudlian fan attempting to scratch an "X" in the box in lieu of his own signature, as presumably required upon his fortnightly visits to the Labour Exchange. And yet, it was Arsenal who were forced to endure the vocal brickbats. Small wonder they were occasionally put off their stroke. Let us cast our mind back to the heyday of twentieth century modernist literature, before the "masses" had crawled out of their chimneys to lower the tone. Virginia Woolf is at her writing table, composing To The Lighthouse. Would she have produced such an elegant tome, ripe for the edification of her many social and intellectual inferiors, had the fans of rival author James Joyce, in a fit of baseness, gathered about her bellowing, "AAAAHHH!!!! SHIT! C'MON JAMES! JOYCE FANS TILL WE DIE! JOYCE FANS TILL WE DIE! CLOSE HER DOWN! DON'T LET HER GET HER HAND ON THE QUILL!! C'MON JAMES! USE YOUR STREAM OF CONSCIOUSNESS! STEAL HER FUCKING INKPOT C'MONNNN!!!!" She would not. Neither, understandably, did Arsenal.

SELF-RIGHTEOUS: There were eleven players on that pitch last night. Pride. Passion. Heart. Commitment. Guts. Honesty (Experience, 65 min). The Shirt. Spittle. The spirit of Stan Boardman. Gerrard. Carragher. All of them, especially the Shirt, were fit to wear the Shirt. They took John Lennon, George Harrison and Brookside from us but they cannot take away our Shirt. What does it represent, the Shirt? To me, to everyone who holds Liverpool Football Club dear, it represents one thing – and that is The Shirt. What Liverpool fan, when the see the Shirt cannot think of the word "Shirt"? Every letter in that hallowed word counts, every letter, like the Liverpool team, plays its part. Take away the "r" and what are you left with? Shit. Makes you think, eh? That tells you everything you need to know about The Shirt. Last night, we were Shirt and you know we were.

HARTLEY: Laughingly, the municipal trough that is Liverpool has been dubbed City of Culture. This "City", whose sole contribution to the gaiety of nations has been the televisual dramas of a Mr Alan Bleasdale (if you count as "drama" men in donkey jackets mumbling unintelligible imprecations at one another as they hatch a plan to steal a spade) and the supposedly popular singing group by the name of The Cockroaches (or some other form of insect infestation; I am too enamoured of Mozart to inquire further into the matter). What is for certain is that, to the eternal shame of we who hold the values of liberty, equality and fraternity dear, the city of Liverpool was founded on the spoils of slave labour. This is an obscene stain upon the conscience. Reparation must be made. But what? Here is my suggestion. That the citizens of Liverpool become our slaves in turn. One per household. It seems, if Mr Bleasdale is any guide, that these people are anxious to find employment – well, we could put them to proper work, tarring our roofs, cleaning our Agas or, of an evening, as simple footstools. There is a spittle problem with these people, but that could be fixed with a small and inexpensive operation, performed at the same time as when they were taken to be spayed. They could live in your stables, subsisting on oats, excreting in the straw. Only by such radical measures can justice for the people of Africa be secured – but who is strong enough to grasp the nettle? Arsenal! Always next season! Or the season after that! Or when we're dead and buried! . . .

SELF-RIGHTEOUS: This result, this represents, quite literally, the renaissance of a city. This reminds everyone what Liverpool is all about. We're supposed to be City Of Culture, right? Well, let's us be having some of them plum jobs, then. Instead of that Russell Davies writing Dr Who, get Carla Lane writing it. Get some of the fun back. "Dalek? I'll Dalek you in a minute!" "Cyberman! I'll Cyberman you in a minute!" We'd be falling about. Instead of that kecks bloke, Paxman, on friggin' Newsnight, get Cilla Black on the job. She'd asks the questions we all want asking of them politicians. ("What's yer name and where d'yer come from?") How's about Margi "Letter To Brezhnev" Clarke starring in a six-part telly drama about Queen Elizabeth I? With Michael Angelis as Sir Walter Raleigh and Tom O'Connor as court jester? ("Remember when you were a kid and your mam used to give you castor oil?") Walk tall! That night in Istanbul! The Shirt!

ENGLAND V ANDORRA (World Cup qualifier)
September 6, 2008

England's first competitive match under Capello sees them uncharacteristically short of ideas in front of a defensive-minded team of part-timers, before Joe Cole saves blushes with a brace.

CLUELESS, CAN'T-BE-ARSED ENGLAND MAKE RIDICULOUSLY HARD WORK OF IT AGAINST COUNTRY WHOSE PRIME MINISTER PROBABLY DOUBLES UP AS LOCAL FUCKING ODD JOB MAN 2-0*

A selection of intriguing and absorbing facts about Andorra, a country which I believe I may have stepped on during a walking tour of Europe in the early 1920s, in order to work off some of the surplus poundage that comes with middle age.

THE last goal Andorra scored was in the year 783. Although this turned out be an own goal, celebrations raged for several weeks as news spread across the tiny Empire, with several goats injured in the course of the revelry.

GOATS were granted the right to vote in Andorra in 1978, three years prior to their women.

DRIED goat's excrement is considered a delicacy in Andorra, though the only foreigner to have tasted the dish, Leonard Woolf, wrote in his journal, "It tastes not unlike dried goat's excrement."

THE best-selling book in Andorra's history was the confessional memoir of a serial goat abuser. Published in 1986, it was entitled My Life In The Bush Of Goats, and sold 28 copies.

Such was the nation who had the snivelling impertinence to range themselves against England's mighty warriors, our emergent Golden Generation upon the field of play last night. The eyes of the world were upon this fixture; it was unwise, certainly, for other nations to stage footballing fixtures of their own concurrent to this one, as their attendances and viewing figures would surely have suffered as a consequence. As for England, cities and towns normally bustling of a Saturday evening were eerily silent, as every man jack and woman jill gathered around wirelesses and television sets to attend to England's performance. And, having watched the game myself in its entirety, once upon television and then twice again on videogram, I can attest that in terms of entertainment, comparisons to standing in the rain watching a wet piece of wood slowly warping would be wholly inappropriate.

The national anthems, as ever, rendered the actual playing of the game an irrelevance. Our men's loins were visibly girded as they pumped out the British anthem, although all of us will have experienced that familiar sense of disappointment as it drew to a close. As for the Andorran equivalent, it resembled little more than an attempt to play the French anthem that got hopelessly lost after the first few bars, resulting in calamity, farce, men in plumed hats colliding with fellows carrying big bass drums, and goat injury. The contrast between our boys, hearty John Bulls one and all, and their ragged, sun-dried opponents was indisputable. England's players are brought to full fighting trim through a sophisticated regimen of training, diet and conditioning. Andorra's men looked like their idea of a training programme was to run round the country six times the day before the match.

As the game commenced, Andorra's strategy became clear. It was to pack their penalty box with as many bodies they could muster – men, women, children, goats – in order to repel the English. No amount of coaxing would induce them to stand aside and allow England to fulfil their manifest destiny, to score goal upon goal unimpeded by querulous foreigners. Every honest attempt on England's part to drive home the ball into the Andorran net was met not with cowed congratulations but shabby sabotage. One recalled the words of the 19th-century poet James Gay, contemplating the mystifying resistance of the Egyptians to British forces. "It seems they are a wicked race/The British flag they don't embrace." Andorra were equally baffling. It was as if they did not want England to score, in spite of the lesson this would teach them. It was as if they had some agenda of their own.

Still, our players pressed on. Stewart Downing should consider changing his name to "Stewart Upping", so top-notch was his performance. That, I should explain, was a play upon words, designed to amuse. Wayne Rooney certainly did not come across like a spoiled, hairy, over-indulged, fat-arsed, spotty teenager who nowadays plays the game as if perpetually on the verge of grabbing the ball and running home with it. As for Frank Lampard, it is hard to think of a superlative that is appropriate for his performance.

It was kind of the FA to allow team mascot Fabio Capello to sit in the dugout for the duration of the game, perhaps as a birthday treat, and what a treat it was as cheeky chappy chirpy cheepy cockney cocksparrer Joe Cole found a way through the packed Andorran population and scored the two goals which ensured victory and ensured that we go with confidence into next Wednesday's fixture against Croatia, or Freedonia, or whatever hastily flung together tinpot principality the buffoons at FIFA have licensed to play football against proper nations. I would, however, wish to issue one caveat, based on tonight's unblemished showing. Given that running about is too vulgar an exertion for a fellow of his stature and note, special dispensation should be granted to allow for David Beckham to be transported about the field during games in a sedan chair, with Theo Walcott and Jermain Defoe as bearers. In return, Mr Beckham might agree to wave to the crowd, and his fellow players, from time to time. Moreover, as opposition players flock to seek his autograph, it would draw them out of position, enabling the likes of Gerrard to blast at goal unimpeded by jealous spoilers.

*NB Seppings: I have a pressing business engagement, concerning my jute interests, and must depart immediately. It is your task to supply a fitting headline for this Report. Then, administer yourself a sound thrashing, on account.

CROATIA V ENGLAND (World Cup qualifier)
September 10, 2008

Against the run of recent games, England shock their nemesis Croatia away from home, with Theo Walcott showing a characteristically sure first touch to grab a hat-trick.

GLORIOUS CHEQUERED WARRIORS OF CROATIA EXPOSE FUNDAMENTAL EFFEMINACY AND IMPURITY OF ENGLAND 1-4

During the Second World War, in my capacity as Field Marshal of the unconquerable Independent Croatian Army, I was wont to slake my thirst with the blood of the benighted Serbs, rank with impurity as it was. Each day, I had my bondsman and manservant Seppic bring to my quarters a bowl of eyeballs, by way of assurance that the slaughter was proceeding satisfactorily. This he did, for he knew that were he to fail in his task, I would slice him to pieces with my sabre where he stood. I recall one occasion when word reached me from my spies of half a dozen members of the English Special Air Squadron who had slipped into the country with a view to undermining Axis interests. I instructed Seppic personally to liquidate these Englishmen, bring proof of their dispatch, or bear the brunt of my sabre tip. The fellow gulped a couple of times, then nodded. It should have been no onerous chore; as we have shown more than once, though the English outnumber us by more than ten to one, we are more than their match upon the field of conflict. And, sure enough, the next day, he produced a bowl of 12 eyeballs, six of which bore monocles. This, to my discerning Croatian mind, was proof perfect that Seppic had succeeded in his task – for the monocle is a precise hallmark of the Englishman, as any competent racial biologist will tell you. Rumours in the ranks that Seppic had merely acquired the eyeballs from the local slaughterhouse and picked up the monocles in a joblot from a Hrvatska flea market were surely unfounded; the glorious legend of the Triumph of the Croatian Will against the mincing, jodhpur-clad English was born. I celebrated by administering Seppic a sound thrashing, which he endured with true Croatian fortitude.

This story has sustained me in my subsequent years, as right-hand man first of Tito, then Tudjman, and today, the present incumbent as Croatia teeters gloriously on the brink of full EEC membership, an organisation which we shall surely come to dominate. You English are soft! You are softened by too few wars and too many vowels. "Rooney"? Have you enough "oo"s there? He would know what we were about when he met our men, scarred by conflict and accents, toughened by clusters of conso-nants which, if any Englishman even tried to utter them, would choke them to death like a foul pig.

The national anthems showed our contrasting mettle. Our own, glorious Croatian anthem, whose full version lasts three and a half weeks, trembles with righteous indignation at the still-warm memories of the Battle Of Mohacs in 1526. The English anthem, by contrast, plods wanly, as if its true lyric should read "We are about to lose/Let's have a cup of tea/We always lose/Rank and inglorious/Eurovision nul points/What is the point of us?/We always lose."

The game commenced at a cracking pelt. To my mind, a good game is one which, like the classic 1990 fixture between Dinamo Zagreb and Red Star Belgrade, triggers a protracted, all-out bloody war. This had all the makings of such a fixture, as several manly challenges attested. Our frontline would surely have scored several goals in the first 15 minutes were they not repulsed by the deeply sexually unattractive countenance of John Terry. The contrast between the English attack and the Croatian defence was notable. Look at little Theo Walcott, a strange-looking specimen, the sort from which our young boys would remove the khaki trousers to see if it had any genitals. He sprinted down the line like a squealing girl running for cover from the corrective and cleansing threat of an oncoming missile attack. Our glorious Croatian defenders did not run after him. We Croatians do not run. Like our back four, we stand, firm and stock still. We stand our ground, for which our forefathers slaughtered the Serbs like filthy goats.

I understand there are numerous homosexuals in the England team. Such a condition, as any truly patriotic biologist will tell you, is un-Croatian. Even though our glorious manager wears an earring, which is known to infect those who wear them with the disease of homosexuality, it has no effect upon him because so cleansed is our Croatian blood that it is immune to such germs. This is what he demonstrates to a watching world. Down with Carnaby Street sodomy!

Come the second half and it was clear that this game was lacking one thing – blood. Hence, Robert Kovac's challenge on Joe Cole, who fainted like a small, petticoated girl overcome by the mere sight of a war grave. Now, we had blood! The blood which cleanses and purifies us! This was where the game was won. Goals are for girls – the men-girls of England.

Glorious as this result was, it might have been even more glorious if we collected together into some sort of federation with our accursed neighbouring countries, and pooled together our greatest players, overlooking their racial inferiority if at least they had some basic clue how to overcome a laughing stock like England, of all teams. We could call it "Yugoslavia" or something. After the 2010 World Cup, we could disband the federation – this would involve a protracted and complex European war, but no matter. War is good! It hardens and purifies us. It cleanses. It inspires.

ENGLAND V KAZAKHSTAN (World Cup qualifier)
October 11, 2008

With countless uncharacteristically unfunny Borat jokes on the various sports channels ringing in their ears, England eventually run out easy winners in this home fixture despite being held to 0-0 at half time. There are concerns about the orchestrated negativity of sections of the England support. An entertaining performance is capped by a spectacular error from Ashley Cole.

ENGLAND'S EXEMPLARS THRASH HALF STARVED DOGS OF KAZAKHSTAN 5-1

There is a reason why England lies at the centre of the world, with the remainder of the planet's countries looking on with baleful envy from the periphery, shamefully aware of just how far, far away they are. We are a country that knows itself, its customs, its history. Since the days of King Egbert, we have been a country that always knew how to stage a truly splendid and colourful civil war, whose marvellous idea of passing the time is in pursuits such as pancake-tossing and stick-waving. Contrast this with our foes this day, Kazakhstan. This is a nation whose people were only officially ratified as human thanks to a majority vote in the United Nations in 1997, a nation who for many years used their reserves of oil as a cheap means of dying their moustaches. Their technical pride has been a space launch facility, from which they once fired a man-made rocket in the vague hope that it might land somewhere solid. In the event, it descended three miles short of Uzbekistan. This is a country so new to the ways of the world that it was only the day before the fixture that it occurred to their football association that, in order to participate in a fixture of this nature, it would be necessary to assemble a team. This they did at the last minute, rounding up 15 men who would otherwise have spent their afternoons sitting in rusty chairs in the town square, looking on with fascination at a dog scratching its ear.

The national anthems told their own story. Our own was delivered with customary gusto, prompting one to wonder why it is not annually put forward as our entry in the Eurovision Song Contest. The Kazakh anthem suggested that none of their country's representatives had brought a copy of the sheet music for it since, this being a young country, no one had as yet got around to writing one, obliging the musicians to improvise something anthemic-sounding on the spot.

With the referee having patiently explained to the Kazakh team before the game that players would not be allowed to take to the field on horseback, and that any attempt to eat the football would be regarded as a yellow card offence, all was ready for the game to commence. Once again, England's amusing Italian mascot Signor Capello was allowed in the dugout. His presence there appears to bring the team good luck – doubtless the players take turns to rub his head before the game. There had been talk of team tactics and formation, with some commentators wondering whether it would be a shrewd idea to play Gerrard and Lampard together – and give the remaining nine players a rest until Wednesday's fixture.

The match started at a brisk clip, hampered only by the Kazakhs' fundamental confusion as to the game's etiquette. Rather than standing quietly by on the touchlines applauding respectfully as England marauded across their home turf, they used all manner of cynical, possession-retaining tactics quite foreign to our understanding of the game. One sensed impatience with the Kazakh team growing in the stadium. One wondered, also, why they were not being closely man-marked by eleven immigration officials, keeping a tight watch on these would-be migrants, lest some break from the field and organise a carwashing business, thereby ruining the English economy.

It was a sterling England performance. Theo Walcott turned in a masterclass in the fine art of running around a lot. As for Steven Gerrard, his distribution was another eloquent argument for demolishing Wembley Stadium and rebuilding it with a new pitch measuring 380 yards long and 275 yards wide – a pitch large enough to accommodate the grand scale of his ambitious passing.

Come the second half and the Kazakh team emerged from the tunnel like famished whelps, whimpering in the knowledge of the thrashing that awaited them as punishment for their impertinent first-half display. They attempted to atone by way of the obsequious offering of an own goal, but this was insufficient. England stood glowering over them, chests puffed, smouldering and askance, riding crop in hand, like the master of the house who has chanced upon an economic migrant in his skullery raping his bulldog (as these rascals are wont to do). Goal upon goal was rained upon the Kazakhs for their defiance. They did score themselves, and there are those who have wondered what was going through Ashley Cole's mind as he placed a perfectly weighted pass across his own penalty box to the feet of a Kazakh attacker. Perhaps he was still brooding on the injustice of having played for fully an hour without some accounts clerk having come onto the pitch with a wheelbarrow full of money and deposited it at his feet. It's more likely, however, that he had become exasperated with the Kazakhs' ineptitude in front of goal and decided to lay on a demonstration of the noble art of passing. "This is how you do it, you blundering, sub-Asian dolts!" That the Kazakhs chose to take advantage of his generosity by placing the ball into the net is but further proof of their perfidious ingratitude.

Now, there has been some carping talk concerning those England fans who turned up to the game only to boo. It seems to me that we must not get this out of proportion. This is only football. A measured response is necessary. I therefore propose that those responsible for the booing be identified by CCTV, rounded up, flayed and pilloried, then hung, drawn and quartered, with their disembowelled remains skewered on spikes outside the Tower Of London. Anything sterner than this would, to my mind, be heavy-handed and excessive.

INAPPROPRIATE CHAMPIONSHIP MANAGER reflects on a further series of disappointing results

Vs CRYSTAL PALACE, 0-4 (a)

It wasn't the result we were looking for. But by Heaven, we'll not be throwing in the towel. Sometimes, in this game, like the game of life, people have it in for you and they're screaming for your head. It's a bit like turning up drunk on a visit to Auschwitz. Basically, it's a pre-season tour of Eastern Europe, an opportunity to get some match fitness under our belts but also to unwind, take in the local sights. So off you go to Auschwitz, you've brought a few tins for the coach journey, perhaps not properly paced yourselves and by the time you reach the camp and are shown round, you're singing a few salty songs that may have caused offence, crawling round on your hands and knees and relieving yourselves in a few places the PC brigade would say you perhaps oughtn't have, to be fair. That's football. But I'll tell you this. Like Anne Frank, we're in a battle for our very lives, this club. Thing is, we intend to go one better than Anne Frank. We intend to survive.

Vs SHEFFIELD WEDNESDAY, 1-4

I'll take the positives – it was good for us to register our first goal of the season, even if is was their keeper booting the ball into the back of his own net when he thought he'd heard the final whistle. We kept harrying and that was our reward. But we were impetuous at times today and that's cost us. It's a bit like heroin. You've heard great things about it, so you think, why not give it a go, but on the other hand, it's a class A drug, some people say it has side effects, and that gives pause for thought. So you do the cautious thing, you try it out on your kids first, see how they get along with it. Tell them it's a booster jab or something, you know how they fret at ages eight and ten. And they seem fine, but then there's the comedown, the vomiting and, after a few weeks, well, they're in a bit of a sorry state, addicted quite honestly, and to be fair we've had to kick them out of the house. So, there you are. Be cautious. Because if I'd been impetuous, the way we were out on that park today, it could have been me getting kicked out of the house. There but for the grace of God, as they say.

Vs CHARLTON, 0-5

We've not come away with the points today but we've come away with a certain amount of pride. Because, to be fair, I've had to take a few brickbats over team selection and the close season signings I've made – particularly Nigel Spunktard. Now, there's been all kinds of crazy suggestions about why I signed a player like Nigel Spunktard, unproven at this level, which I won't even dignify with a response in this interview. There's people coming out and saying, you know, is he the latest in a succession of similar signings including Dieter Münchdick, the African lad Joseph Blo Job, Arsene Titz, the Belgian feller Pieter Cunnilingers and the Korean boy Suk Mi Kok. The fact that they're all what in the old days we would have called right-sided wing-backs has raised this ridiculous idea that somehow I signed them because of something to do with their names, and I've left the team lopsided. To which I say, I select my team on merit and merit alone. Which is why even a hot prospect like our South American Jose Luis De Lourdes Enrique Santa Eduardo Cunt can't even get a game just now.

Vs DERBY, 0-3

It's not the result we were looking for, no. I know it, the fans know it, those lads back in that dressing room know it. And to concede all three goals in injury time certainly raises issues about our concentration and focus. We thought we could hold out for a point but that final whistle came just too late for us. It's like, well, we've all been there. You get a rumbling, churning sensation in your bowels and you realise the call of nature is ringing rather urgently. But there's no public convenience immediately to hand so you just hope you can hold it in and weather the storm, so to speak. And the first two or three times you go a bit red, clench the muscles in your hindquarters and you just about manage. But then, the fourth time, the rumbling comes with a vengeance and this time the mudslide won't be denied. It's all the more unfortunate that you're sitting on the face of the chairman's wife at the time, under a hedge in the club car park in a discreet dalliance that, to be fair, you'd hope would have gone rather better, all things being equal. You're not happy, she's certainly not happy and as for the chairman, you only hope that he keeps things in proportion and understands that in football, these things happen, and you take them on the chin, or, to be fair, in the case of his dignified lady wife, down the throat, the nostrils and both ear canals. Next time, perhaps we can get things right and it'll be you that gets the result and it's her sitting on your face.

ENGLAND V BELARUS (World Cup qualifier)
October 15, 2008

A characteristically unwobbly start to this qualifying campaign continues, with two goals from Rooney ensuring England maintain a 100% record against potentially tricky away opposition. A late, howling miss from Gerrard.

ENTERPRISING ENGLAND ROUNDLY SPANK BELARUS BUTTOCKS 3-1

Seaside holidays – that is the difference between England and Belarus, a nation who's official ranking is currently 17th Most Inferior People. Seaside holidays – charabancs, wurlitzers, candy floss, sitting in sweltering temperatures of 17 degrees in deckchairs in three-piece suits, rusty piers that might at any moment fall into the sea with a cheerful splash, the odour of donkeys, the grey sea washing up the occasional consignment of human excrement, every one a fine example of the robustness and healthy colouring of the Great British Stool. Belarus, by contrast, is a landlocked country. Of the seaside, and all of its hale and bracing character-building qualities, they know nothing. If they were presented with a wurlitzer, they would probably attempt to till a field with it; if they saw a charabanc, they would probably surrender to it. It is, after all, common knowledge that Belarus put in an exceptionally poor performance during World War II. Their mortality rates were amusingly high; some 90% of their population was wiped out in the conflict. Being landlocked, and it apparently occurring to none of their obtuse citizens to hide in the forest, they were like fish in a barrel. The very pitch upon which this game was played is, in all probability, a mass grave.

The match took place in the city of Minsk. It is a curious weakness of my manservant Seppings that he giggles uncontrollably whenever the word Minsk is mentioned. I cannot account for the faintly scatological quality he divines in the word, for despite the thrashings I administer to him for open and insubordinate signs of amusement, he cannot help himself.

It is, of course, an outrage that England's players were expected to perform in Belarus at all, given the extent to which radiation from the Chernobyl calamity has seeped across Belarus's borders since 1986. One could see the visible effects in the hideous appearances of Wes Brown, visibly mutating, in Rio Ferdinand, his lips practically melting from his face, and in particular Wayne Rooney, skin blotched, degenerating into the grotesque resemblance of some unholy synthesis of gorilla and fruit as the game wore on. It takes more than a little radiation-induced deformity to put off our English boys, however, and once they had yodelled their way through the national anthem (the Belarus team sang theirs with the hangdog resignation of a country aware that a plate of salt for dinner and sexual inter-course with their tractors is as good as their lives are going to get), the game commenced.

England at once showed their mettle with an early goal converted by Steven Gerrard, who deceived the boatmen stationed outside the stadium who, seeing him shaping up to shoot on the big screen, immediately put out to water. However, Belarus demonstrated their perversity with an equaliser which ran contrary to the English way of playing the game. Twenty-three passes were involved in its build-up. This is not football, this is secession – the same national impulse which impelled Belarus to declare independence from Russia in order that they could be free to elect their own President for Life. Twenty-three passes! No English team could play thus – there would be a deadly build-up of blood, spunk and thunder in our loins. The urge for some player or other to scream John Bull and boot the ball pointlessly into the stands would, quite rightly, prove irresistible. This is what we give the world: our very seed, copiously strewn.

Come the second half and England continued to press, with Emile Heskey playing his appropriate, subordinate role alongside Rooney's roving Robinson Crusoe. Superstars were in the making – England have had their Upsons and Downings over the years, but who can compare with Wayne Bridge? Belarus wilted like famished kulaks whose only meal had been a shared bucket of potash at half time. The goals rained in, with Gerrard almost adding a fourth with a speculative shot from one yard out. With all of several minutes to go, however, and only ahead by a mere two goals, it was absolutely vital that David Beckham be brought on to replenish England's ragged forces, as opposed to parade around the pitch milking the sycophantic applause like The Duke Of Fucking Edinburgh at Ascot, all but wearing a fucking top hat.

Two things emerge from this fixture. The first is that, with England having self-evidently won the 2010 World Cup, the farce of these qualifying group matches should be brought to a halt, lest FIFA suffer the embarrassment of other group games worldwide being played before near-empty stadia, as apathetic performances reflect the international mood, which is to say, "What's the point? All this and they haven't even played Michael Carrick yet. They've got it in the bag."

The second is the growing concern surrounding John Terry, our captain and pillar, and his occasional lapses of fitness for key fixtures. The doctors are baffled; I, however, have prepared a potion which, if taken in pint measures, could hasten his recoveries. It consists essentially of bulldog semen with a dash of nutmeg. I admit that tests have not proven its efficacy beyond medicinal doubt. However, I do believe that its placebo effect alone could prove a fillip to young Mr Terry, if he were to imbibe it with the proper enthusiasm. Dear God, is there nothing this man would not do for his country?

ENGLAND V GERMANY (Friendly)
November 19, 2008

A few major names missing from this Berlin fixture, with domestic club concerns perhaps uncharacteristically high on the agenda. John Terry is both villain and hero, blundering in defence but heading the winning goal against poor opposition.

EVIDENTIALLY SUPERIOR ENGLAND BIFF GERMANY IN WORLD WAR SIX 2-1

It will come as little surprise to those who are acquainted with me, be it through my memoirs, through the capacity of servitude or simply having been on the sharp end of my riding crop for some impertinence or other, that I am strongly inclined to take a dim view of the German people, as those of my generation are wont to. I refer, naturally, to the 1970s, when the country recoiled into a barbarism without precedent in its recent history. This was the era in which all the talk was of the Baader Meinhof and the like, when the Germans, once proud, clipped, erect, properly suspicious of usury in their midst, fell victim to a queer, hirsute madness. I myself was taken hostage in 1972 during a visit to the city of Düsseldorf, where I was due to meet with a certain claque of middle aged, discreet sympathisers in a certain Bierkeller, entry to which could be obtained by uttering the password "Wessel". Owing to a surfeit of Schnapps partaken in my hotel room, however, I found myself suddenly short of bearings in my unsteady perambulations around the town, and ushered into a dark, shadowy basement in which I was forced to sit cross-legged and endure a torture beyond the imagination of less hardened civilians - I was made to listen to a fellow in a headband play the flute at me for what seemed like three days, without sleep.

I was eventually released, thanks no doubt to the intervention of the SAS. However, representatives of the German police fabricated the assurance that I had inadvertently stumbled into a pop concert of some sort by a collective of musicians of the so-called "Krautrock" genre, that the flute solo to which I had alluded had lasted a mere three hours, reasonable for the times, and that it had only been terminated upon my shooting the tanktopped perpetrator in the knee with my service revolver, for which the group themselves had had the brass gall to press charges. Fortunately, since Seppings, my manservant, had wrested the revolver from my hand following my discharging of it, it was decided in open court that his fingerprints proved he had been the one to fire the bullet in question and, white man that he is, he bore the brunt of the subsequent prison sentence. The slightly pained gait with which he walks to this day can be ascribed to his period in that Teutonic gaol, where the social lives of inmates was questionable, to say the least, and lubricants were often in painfully short supply, even on the black market.

It was against this chaotic, seething backdrop of confusion and antipathy that this fixture took place. The national anthems told their own story. The home fans booed our rendition - resentful, perhaps, that we had borrowed and then refused to return the epitome of charm that is the Germany-derived royalty – while the German anthem was intoned by their team with all the hollowness of the already thrice vanquished. Each umlaut was winced, reminding of Seppings during his incarceration anticipating another perilous visit to the communal showers.

There was criticism of the import of this game, a certain downplaying of its undoubted historical significance – I can think of no recent international political event which has had more resonance than this fixture, or whose outcome was more keenly anticipated by a watching world. However, it is no exaggeration, but rather an imaginative simile, to compare this game to World War II – World War II, that is, minus the participation of Churchill, Field Marshall Montgomery, Adolf Hitler, Herman Goering, and Douglas Bader, who, like our own, absent Frank Lampard, suffered from the handicap of not being able to use his legs in any effective way.

My one regret upon watching this game was that the England team did not line up and deliver, as they did in 1938, the Nazi salute before the start of the game. No doubt the political correctness of the liberal elite quashed this sensible proposal. However, it would have had the felicitous effect of wiping the slate of the 1940s clean, signifying a new beginning based upon the happy assumption that the events of 1939-45 never happened. Certainly, viewing the German team's first half performance in particular, one entertained the thought that if this had been the best they could muster back in 1939, they would have been as well off restricting their global military adventures to running to the Czech border, throwing pebbles at the guards on patrol, then swiftly running away again, leather shorts squeaking with fretfulness between their thighs. Tonight's was not a great vintage.

As for England, their every onslaught had the Germans scurrying about in a somewhat pitiful, cry-baby panic, the way their citizens did in Dresden in 1944 (in similar circumstances, John Bull, his wife Joan and their children Johnny and Joanetta would doubtless have stood in the streets, square jawed, waving their fists in contempt at the oncoming Dorniers). It was no surprise when we went ahead – by this point, the Germans would have had a better chance against Blighty in a joke-telling or irony-getting or sunbed-reserving-fairly competition. Come the second half and only Darren Bent's inability to stay upright on a wet surface prevented England from attaining a second goal. Instead, in a calamity of which more later, the Germans fortuitously gained parity. Thankfully, John Terry, our captain, headed the winner with but minutes to spare. Seppings, bending over to serve me upon a platter a flagon of restorative brandy, bore the brunt of my appreciation. He is under strict instructions not to wash his face for a fortnight.

I should like to raise a practical point at this juncture. It would, I'd warrant, prove a psychological boost to our boys were England to stage an open bus-top victory celebration for the 2010 World Cup early in the new year, with Gary Neville and David Beckham holding aloft the trophy, whether sanctioned by FIFA or obtained by the SAS from their headquarters, as the bus wends its slow way through Regent Street towards Trafalgar Square. This would make further sense in that many families would be taking their summer holidays in July, when the competition proper is scheduled to finish, and would therefore miss the subsequent parade.

A word too about John Terry. It will not have escaped the notice, not least of carping naysayers, that he was arguably, fractionally to blame for the defensive mishap which led to Germany's goal tonight. I know Terry, shaped as he is from the hard knocks of head against tarmac while playing British Bulldog in the streets as a child, is his own, fiercest critic and, if unsupervised, is liable to descend into a negative spiral of heated self-excoriation for his supposed mistake. In order to avert this, I urge that for his own good, and for that of his team and country, he is confined to a padded room, bound to a chair in a straitjacket and a bucket of water thrown in his face every 15 minutes by a male orderly. Just until the next England fixture, at any rate. Yes, I thought so too.

ENGLAND V SPAIN (Friendly)
February 11, 2009

England's recent winning run and subsequent euphoria is tempered by this away setback against the European champions and world's number one ranked team. Another player uncharacteristically surnamed Cole gets a game.

BOLD ENGLISH BULLDOGS SCRATCH AWAY SPANISH FLEA
0-2

The Spanish have been in boastful mood of late, having won some spurious continental trophy of some sort over the summer period. That no team from the British Isles appears to have contested this competition, however, shows it up for the worthless, oversized bauble it is. No doubt Spain are also the cricketing champions of their geographical region, having seen off stiff competition from the Portuguese, Italians and Albanians. It is of laughably little matter. Tonight, they would understand that there is a reason why the backbone of the average Spaniard is some 30 degrees shy of the happy ideal enjoyed by the more evolutionary erect English. This was Homo Sapiens versus Homo Spaniardum.

The game took place in Seville, though the acclaimed barber of that city has some explaining to do, since the coiffure of the Spanish reminded of some of the worst excesses of Crufts (Most Preposterously Primped Poodle category) in the more licentious years of the late 20th century. Tonight, however, there was several minutes' delay before these benighted foreigners took to the field. There was John Terry, chest puffed, nostrils flaring, hooves scraping, champing at the bit, heading up the England eleven in the tunnel. The Spaniards, however, took no little while to emerge. There can only be one explanation for this: abject, Iberian terror. One imagines a representative of the English FA bursting into the dressing room of these cowering, curly-haired recalcitrants and bellowing at them to emerge from under their tables, like an apoplectic Basil Fawlty screaming at Manuel to help him deposit the pyjama-ed body of a recently deceased hotel guest into a laundry basket, on pain of a damn good thrashing.

Ironically, it is England who could have delayed their entry to the field by 20 minutes, finished a game of crown green bowls at their hotel and still carried the day. It is an interesting historical fact that Sir Francis Drake was not considered a particularly notable or adept military man by English standards. Had he been born in the 17th as opposed to the 16th century and taken part in a domestic campaign such as our own, splendid English Civil War, he would probably have found it hard to find a place in either side. However, given that the task of defeating the Spanish Armada was such a footling one, it was charged to him, lowly ranked underling that he was. So it was this evening. This being only Spain, we did not bother sending out our first-rank players. Had this game taken place a week later, during half term, we might have sent out our schoolboys or even Ladies' XI, but this being what is known as a "school night", both had homework studies and maternal duties respectively to attend to.

As it was, we did, whimsically, select players from the regions, including a brace from a team known as Aston Villa whom, Seppings informs me, play their football in the West Midlands district and are considered enthusiastic players, in a capering, amusing sort of way. Hence the inclusion of one Agbonlahor, whose expression during the formalities – squinting, quizzical, mouthbreathing – gave the impression of one who would require directions in finding his way from the touchline onto the pitch. One congratulates him on his effort to sing the national anthem, much as one congratulates a dog that, after patient training, is fitfully able to bark the word "sausages". As for the Spanish anthem, it was sheer, orchestrated abjection. It was conducted at the brisk, marching pace of an army division exiting their barracks in formation at the double, but then, upon being informed that they were going to war against the Maltese, returning with equal speediness back to their quarters to lock themselves in the latrines.

The match itself showed the gulf between the English and Spanish way of conducting themselves upon the field of play. There is a fine line between deft interplay and grown men making a series of passes at one another which is homosexualist in the extreme. Regrettably, the Spaniards breached that line constantly. Not like our own boys, who delivered the ball to one another with a manly vigour, the equivalent of a hearty, phlegm-loosening slap on the back which reverberates through bowels and testicles alike and affirms English manhood. Thus did Johnson pass to Heskey, Terry to Downing.

The anomalous scoreline at half time can be attested to be a series of shabby decisions on the part of the referee, a Frenchman, no less. It was either a crass blunder or an act of imprisonable corruption on the part of the authorities to appoint an official from the same continent as the Spaniards, similarly mired in the sewer of palm grease that is their common element. Small wonder that England were unsettled, culminating in, of all things, an error by David James – an event as rare as a British military blunder or a lapse in good taste on the part of the Royal Family. "Where were you the night David James dropped the ball?" fans shall ask of one another, decades hence.

Come the second half and the big guns were trundled out in the form of Peter Crouch, Frank Lampard and David Beckham, enjoying his 108th cap for England. Among those they replaced were Jagielka, who has 107 caps to look forward to. Lampard's performance can be summed up in one word. Fewer, in fact. Further reinforcements came with the addition of Carlton Cole. For those who say, "For fuck's sake, just because some slow-moving, goal-hanging lummox, whom the ball occasionally bounces off in the fucking six yard box into the net through no ingenuity of his own happens to be called fucking Cole, do we have to put him in the fucking England team?", he provided the perfect riposte, by blasting a ball from six yards out directly into the press box, a magnificent rejoinder to his detractors. A few minutes later, the Spanish grabbed a late consolation goal and time was eventually called. This was plainly an unequal match. On the one hand, a nation who had the get-up-and-go to acquire an Empire within recent, living memory, pitted against a nation who haven't even managed to conquer their own country outright as yet, let alone anyone else's. Small wonder that Spain experienced a "reality check" in this confrontation with their footballing, physical, social and genetic superiors, the English.

HUGH MCLAUGHTON, BROADSHEET CORRESPONDENT

WHAT IS TO BE DONE ABOUT ALL THESE CRYING MILLIONAIRE WOMEN?

They say a woman is a costly commodity and, as one whose patience with the comelier sex has oft been put to the utmost strain, I find that I cannot but concur. Ask anyone from any profession, be they sportswriter, executive editor, or senior manager in any field and they will tell you the same tale of woe - of the perfumes, stoles, and assorted fineries they have had to lavish, the milliner's bills they have had to run up, in order to placate their wives and thereby preserve their conjugal rights, as must be demanded when stumbling in at three in the morning after a fortifying dram. "Women," as the old Scottish sage Wilfred O' Muchterlauchty once put it in phrases hewn from the granite of his infinite wisdom, "are the apples of God's eye. But they're also the scum of the earth. Painted whores, every one of them, destined for the Inferno. Remember that, laddie. Aye, yer mother too."

One wonders what that good man O' Muchterlauchty, who died at the ripe old Scottish age of 37, would have made of the women of today? I speak, of course, of those roundly rebuked from the very heights of Ministerial Office, to wit, the likes of John Terry, Wayne Rooney, Cristiano Ronaldo, women indeed to a man as sure as gruts are gruts, who earn, according to ministerial figures, roughly one million pounds a day to act the perfumed pansy upon the too-pristine pitch, while to the North, the men of Govan are forced to forage on slagheaps in order to fill their coal bunkers for the coming winter.

Where is the passion of yore? The grit? The gruts? The granite? The grime? The gruel? One casts one's mind back over the sadly elapsed decades to more straitened but economically rational times, in which footballer's benevolent, tophatted paymasters did not have to abide to the behest of greasy, swarthy Shylocks, or "agents" (one hesitates to call them "Jews") in order to decide how best to reward their footballing charges with the money they had honestly accrued, thanks to the industrial revolution being, fortunately, not a revolution of the Russian sort. One thinks of the Potter Brothers, men of their word, for whom a spit and a handshake was worth more than any contract. When they signed young Stanley Matthews in 1932, they offered him the then princely sum of one shilling and sixpence a week, ample enough for a young lad to make a trip to the Flicker Gallery, feast on a Knickerbocker Glory then catch the last tram home. When he retired in 1965, the Potter Brothers showed their consistency and their moral mettle. The deal had been sewn up as surely as the leather casing on a football. Despite his advanced age, they did not reduce his wage by a single farthing. A shilling and sixpence a week was the deal in 1932 and a shilling and sixpence was the deal 33 years on, plus all the dubbin he needed to keep those wizard's boots to a high shine.

One thinks also of wee Archie McGaughlicuddy, the "Mercury Midget", the 4'6" Wonder Winger whose jinking runs would guarantee near-sellout gates of 320,000 at Parkhead when he turned out in the green hoops of Glasgow Celtic. The munificence of Harry Protheroe, the somewhat autocratic but fundamentally benign chairman and bankroller of the great club, was appropriate. He saw to it that the millions of pounds of revenue generated by McGaughlicuddy's magical caperings did not go unacknowledged. To that end, when a reckless fondness for gobstoppers saw the winger turfed out of lodgings, his sweet tooth precluding him from keeping up with the pound a month rent, Mr Protheroe (as he was known to his close friends and wife Agnes) saw to it that McGaughlicuddy was put up on his very own estate – in Mr Protheroe's very own coal bunker, to be precise. There, away from the temptations of the confectioner's store, McGaughlicuddy thrived. The more so, I should hasten to append, because he received from the great and goodly Mr Protheroe personally the finest advice he would ever receive in his life. "If the yen for a gobstopper takes you," said the furlined Captain Of Industry, "suck on a lump of coal instead." This the tiny winger took to heart. (Sadly, he died, aged 26, of coal poisoning, the way many a good Scotsman met his Maker back in those terrible, wonderful, terrible, wonderful days.)

Show the likes of a John Terry a tin of dubbin and she would doubtless apply it to her hair. Show Cristiano Ronaldo a lump of coal and advise her to make a meal of it rather than those manly challenges she clatters in a heap to of a week, and she would probably have to be revived by her agent with smelling salts. The Inferno surely awaits both these ladies . . .

ENGLAND V SLOVAKIA (Friendly)
March 28, 2009

A routine warm-up for the World Cup Qualifier against Ukraine, with Rooney excelling in front of goal. England sport a new, almost virginally all-white kit. Skrtel has a nightmare for the Slovaks, while John Terry makes one or two uncharacteristic errors of his own, including denying Crouch a goal by heading in his netbound shot while offside.

IMPECCABLE ENGLAND SKEWER SLOVENLY SLOVAKIAN SWINE 4-0

As England's men took to the field of play clad in extreme white, their spotless shorts a glowing testimony to English detergents, the envy of a grubby globe, one's lip curled on contemplating our opponents this evening: the Slovakians, now half the country they once were and showing it in their barren, dead-eyed countenances, struggling to pronounce even their own names. Here was a nation who were the last, the very last in Europe to acquire independence – in 1993, no less. Let us delve deeper into their history. As recently as 1241, they were invaded by the Mongols.

The Mongols, I ask you. Had a single defending British garrison been on hand in such a contingency, they would have made short work of such an incursion, by the simple expedient of breaking open a barrel of tin tacks, strewing them across the national border, then looking on with amusement from the turrets as the onrushing, barefooted Mongol mob suddenly began hopping about in agony before beating a painful retreat to their pagodas. But then, as a certain Mr Skrtel demonstrated this evening, defence is hardly the Slovakians' strong point.

The national anthems were a further demonstration of the biological advantages enjoyed by the English over their foes, not least in the matter of washing powder. Our own, as ever, aroused a wistful, rheumy sensation in the eyes and a surge in the plus-fours. As for the Slovakian effort, it raises the entire question of why national anthems are dished out so willy-nilly to any Tom, Dick or Balkan who decides, out of pique, to secede. But then, our own anthem is the musical embodiment of the English dream – one of invention, enterprise, tea and scones and sensible dominion over the ethnically troublesome and minerally naïve. Here, by contrast, is a nation who dream of one day packing themselves like sardines into a container lorry and smuggling themselves into England, living high on the hog at our expense, cleaning cars 23 hours a day.

And so, while their womenfolk, their "WAGS" to use the parlance, busied themselves shopping at some of South England's most notable car boot sales, the Slovakians entered into the footballing fray. In truth, the match ought to have been called off after a few minutes. Diet was the key to the Slovakian sluggishness – subsisting as they do on blood sausages, boiled cucumbers and horses' testicles, it was clear that they would be no match for a Wayne Rooney, he whose sleek contours bespeak a sound attitude to food consumption. It was no surprise when England took an early lead. It was unfortunate that Heskey should have sustained an injury in scoring the goal – however, he was replaced "like for like", negro for negro, with Carlton Cole. Here, then, we had an interesting situation, with two players by the name of "Cole", Ashley and Carlton, upon the field of play. I had intended at this point to leaven this report with a humorous observation based upon this particular coincidence. However, I am informed that were I to do so, it would be expurgated. And so, unhappily, you will have no idea as to the nature of the joke I would have assayed.

Come the second half, and a further series of injuries, very possibly the result of Slovakian old wives' sorcery, damn their headscarves, left England bereft of an attacking force, with first Carlton Cole and then Peter Crouch (or "Peedah" Crouch, as it appears his name is properly pronounced, according to that excellent authority Mr Clive Tyldesley) being forced to leave the field of play. I am sure that Michael Owen, as an Englishman, must feel a swell of pride in knowing that, such is England's strength in depth, with Michael Carrick to call upon as a substitute replacement, or failing him, Stuart Pearce, or falling him, Miss Kelly Smith of Arsenal Ladies, that there is no need for his services.

As the players walked off, the English to thunderous applause, the Slovakians to a detention camp outside Luton prior to their deportation, it occurred to me that it is quite absurd that the momentum of these important England internationals is scuppered by the insistence on playing several rounds of Premier League fixtures at a time in between them. Surely these fixtures could be postponed, or even abandoned altogether?

Some ignorant observers might have considered it the height of bloody-minded, arsefaced Chelsea cockness for our captain, John Terry, to have denied Crouch what would have been a certain goal by lunging in from an offside position and attaching himself to the ball, thereby causing it to be disallowed. This is to misunderstand the player's proper sense of hierarchy. The goal had to go through the proper channels. As captain, only he had the authority within the six-yard box to score the goal. Better that it not be allowed at all than be registered to an insubordinate junior acting recklessly on his own initiative. There must be rules, regulations, and these must be applied rigidly, as a team, as a country, otherwise we too might become two half-nations, separated into "Great" (London, certain of the Home Counties) and "Britain" (the rest).

ENGLAND V UKRAINE (World Cup Qualifier)
April 1, 2009

A key victory, which continues England's remarkable 100% record, with John Terry once again decisive at either end. However, manager Capello's stern expression suggests he is taking nothing for granted. Frank Lampard gives an interview in which he encapsulates the Capello ethos.

INVINCIBLE ENGLAND TAN HIDES OF NUCLEAR BUNGLERS UKRAINE 2-1

"Everyone has an opinion on England – quite rightly so because we're all English." So said Frank Lampard, in a recent interview as he reflected upon the uninterrupted excellence that has been England's natural element since the Bayeux tapestry. This was an especially apt comment, given that it came in the course of his extolling the lack of complacency that characterises the current national team. He is right. We are, of course, all English. You, me, Lampard, every last man of us. However, tonight upon the field of play, there were eleven exceptions, foul and hirsute and clad in the sort of yellow and blue that had them resemble unhelpful shop-floor employees in a large furniture store rather than a team of association footballers.

What can be said of the Ukrainians, whose history has been

spent being battered from pillar to post by every Pole, Slav, Russky and Mongol within invading distance? One has mixed feelings. On the one hand, some of their more enterprising citizens joined forces with the Germans in World War II. They apparently made excellent guards at the settlement camps, asking only a bowl of borscht a month and freedom to use the inmates as chew toys for their Alsatians. All well and good in happier circumstances, but tonight they were pitted against Englishmen. You. Me. Us.

It is a scandal that they were not immediately deducted a goal for the inadequacy of their national anthem, which resembled little else than two tractors following a collision, engines still revving. But then, this is barely a nation, more a tract of contaminated land which its citizens would give many potatoes to leave for good. Small wonder the country, and this is no "April Fool" jape, has its own National Space Agency. Escape by rocketship is the national dream. However, their greatest success thus far has been to launch a missile 86 feet into the air in 1992. It landed on an outside latrine, inconveniencing an entire village for several months. Not like our own, glorious space mission involving a plucky fellow with a beard and an intelligence-gathering projectile, which only overshot Mars by several hundred thousand miles, not unlike a speculative shot from Mr Steven "G" Gerrard.

The game kicked off and England warily assessed their opponents, sizing up their options – to trounce them or to thrash them? Our forward line bamboozled them with deft interplay, like a magician confusing a curious dog with the old balls and cups trick. Inevitably, after toying with these blotchy, beetroot-addled wretches for a while, England struck, courtesy of Peter Crouch. He is apt, as we have seen, when essaying a bicycle kick, to resemble a swastika, and this clearly had the effect of freezing certain elements within the Ukrainian team in rapt deference. It is a good option to have upfront.

Come the second half, and England continued to dominate, so much so that Gerrard could afford to sit out much of the remainder of the match, occasionally mouthing to his teammates, "Come 'ed! Pash it to me? Eh? Pash it! Pash it! Eh? Eh? Besht player in the weeeeeaald, me, they reckon. Berra than Meshi. Come 'ed!" Ashley Cole's touch was as unerroneous as the decision by his publishers to award him a large advance for his memoirs. Gareth Barry put in a performance that hummed to the vibrant rhythm of the West Midlands. However, it was Wayne Rooney who caught the eye in particular. In 1986, the Chernobyl nuclear reactor in the Ukraine exploded, causing 56 deaths and countless cases of cancer. Had Wayne Rooney been a Ukrainian, the problem would have been solved in a trice. Once the conflagration had started, he would simply have run around, dementedly, ill-advisedly, and stamped on it.

England's second goal was simply a matter of inevitability. However, it does raise a matter of great concern, to wit, the reaction of England's mascot, Signor Capello. He reacted with what seemed like ambivalence, even a treacherous chagrin, to both goals. It was as if he was saying, "Ees shame, why ees foreigners no score? I foreigner, I no like." The man must remember that his function in the England set-up is not to provide tacit sympathy to our opponents, but comic relief. Certainly, with his large chin and ill-fitting spectacles he is reasonably amusing-looking but, for future key fixtures, rather than look on stoically, he should be coerced, with menaces if necessary, into a show of Mediterranean exuberance involving high-pitched noises, a unicycle, castanets and kissing a nearby police dog full on the lips in amusing error.

Then there is John Terry, awarded man of the match – mistakenly, in my view. Not because he was at fault for the Ukrainian equaliser, going missing when Shevchenko rifled it in unmarked, or for what a traitorous nitpicker might describe as various crass errors and pointless little fouls that helped make sure the evening was hard work. Rather, because he ought to have been given the award before, not after the game. His, however, was the Captain's Goal with which he earned his champagne. And let there be no doubt that I myself matched the fizzy effervescence upon that bottle's uncorking, as Seppings, who was buffing my spats to a high shine at the time and happened to upturn his face as the ball hit the back of the net, can attest . . .

TOMMY SUNDERLAND, NEWCASTLE UNITED SUPPORTER

In May 2009, Newcastle United are finally relegated, despite the emergency efforts of interim manager Alan Shearer and despite a team of high-earning star players who, it is feared, might not stick around at the club for very long. TOMMY SUNDERLAND reflects cheerfully on a dismal season – and contemplates a change of name.

Howay! Tommy Sunderland here, reporting, like. Actually, I say Tommy Sunderland, but I've a story concerning my name, which I think you'll find quite entertaining but I'll leave it till later on.

Anyway, 2008-09. Certainly a season to remember! It had everything - tragedy, comedy, despair, laughter, tears of misery, tears of amusement. Everything but the kitchen sink. A bit like my house. That doesn't have a kitchen. Or a sink. But like the man said, at the end of the day, I get by, you know, I jog along. If I'm down, I think of Kevin Keegan. If he'd just walked away at the first sign of trouble, where do you think he'd be today? Or Newcastle United football club? Exactly. I should be ashamed of myself.

I'm not going to crow either. Yes, we finished the season above Middlesbrough, so we've got local bragging rights there but I'm not going to get too big-headed about it. Not too smug, like. Oh aye, the 'Boro had a terrible season but ours wasn't perfect either, if I'm completely honest. To be fair, "wor" Alan

Shearer had a mountain to climb when he agreed to come back and manage this club, like the Prodigal Son back from down South and the bright lights and cockney characters, back to the coin-operated meters and cobbled terraces of Newcastle. And he very nearly did it, too. Just a single point he missed out by. Talk about a mountain to climb – that's a bit like almost climbing Mount Everest but having to give up with just a foot to go. That's how close we were to glory. That's how close Alan took us to the mountain top. No wonder they compared him to Jesus. The number of times you'd be in the stands and hear the words "Jesus Christ!!" during the games Alan was in charge. (Actually, he's Mr Shearer to me.) I tell you, some of his tactical formations would have worked if it weren't for that rule about not being allowed to field up to 15 players on the pitch.

Anyway, one thing you can't accuse our players of is lack of effort. They gave 110%. Actually, I know, you can't literally, like, give 110% but our players found a way around that. They gave 100% in some games, 10% in others, you know, as a sort of top up. That's the Toon spirit. Anyway, like the man said, at the end of the day, it's all about the players. They're the ones who wear the shirt, not us, the fans, especially when it gets warm around February time. And so, as a tribute to them, like, here's Tommy's Roll Of Honour, a tribute to the key players who made 2008-09 a season that lived up to all the traditions of Newcastle United FC.

MICHAEL OWEN. Say what you like about the little feller – all right, so he doesn't score goals the way he used to but you can't have everything. He's certainly a presence in the box. The last thing a footballer loses is the capacity to take up space and he certainly does that, more so with each season. They talk about money this and money that but Michael Owen, well, he's the sort of player who'd play for nothing each week, he loves the game that much. I mean, what's he on, £90,000, £100,000 a week? What you've got to remember is that to a feller like Michael Owen, that sort of money practically is nothing, so in a way you could say he is playing for nothing already. I mean, a feller like me, I'll most likely not earn £90,000 in my entire life, but Michael Owen . . . you look at it like that, and you can forgive him looking a bit uninterested now and again. But he's still a danger man – I'd hate to be a Scunthorpe United defender next season!

DAMIEN DUFF. I tell you, it continues to astonish and surprise me, like, that a player of the calibre of Damien Duff can be attracted to play for a club like Newcastle. Sometimes, I'll be watching a game like, and it's deep in the second half and I say to myself, "My God, Damien Duff's on the pitch!" To them naysayers who reckon a clockwork Toby jug on castors would be more use than "wor" Damien, I say – we signed him for £5 million. In 68 games he's already scored four goals and it can only be a matter of months before he bags a fifth. When he does, we'll be able to say that each of those goals is worth a million pounds. And so they are.

MARK VIDUKA. I was a bit peckish the other day, like, so I went and stood outside Greggs the bakers, you know, to get the smell, and some for some reason, funny how the mind works, pastries got me thinking of ""wor" Mark Viduka. What a servant he's been. Cut him and he'd bleed black and white. Only I wouldn't advise it, like, because the wound'd probably put him in the treatment room for nine months. I'm in danger of losing count of the number of goals the big marksman's knocked in for us in just two seasons. But not just yet. It's seven. Like the wonders of the world.

JOEY BARTON. A lot's been said about our resident scamp and loveable rogue Joey Barton – but I say, every man deserves a second chance. After all, Joey gave us a second goal this season, after he'd scored his first goal for the club last season. We should return the favour. Like the man said, at the end of the day, fair's fair.

ALAN SMITH. 39 appearances, no goals as yet. That statistic speaks for itself – here's a man who never stops trying. After all, that's the hardest thing of all, is trying. That's why they talk about "trying hard" and not "succeeding hard". So fair dos to the lad. It's players like him who'll get us back where Newcastle used to be in the glory days of Joe Harvey, Bobby Moncur and Pop Robson – in Division One.

Anyway, like I was saying, about me name, like. I've not been quite happy with it for a while, you know, so I thought, I'll save up for a few months and go down to the Registry Office and get me name changed, you know, to "Newcastle". So that's what I did this morning, and here I am now, it's official, in the council books and all that, da-daa! Yours truly, Newcastle Sunderland! I always hated the name "Tommy". Used to have the mickey taken out of it at school 'cos of that rock group album. Anyway, it's paid dividends already. I used to get beaten up on a weekly basis on account of my name but now it's down to once a fortnight. Onward and Upward with the Toon Army . . .

ENGLAND V ANDORRA (World Cup Qualifier)
June 10, 2009

England extend their remarkable 100% record against Andorra in all recent games to take a further giant stride before 2010. With the task complete before half time, Capello can afford to substitute Gerrard and Rooney.

EFFERVESCENT ENGLAND PUT MISERABLE ANDORRAN MINNOWS TO THE BROADSWORD 6-0

And so, following the relatively small beer of the European

Champions League Final and the FA Cup Final, the last and undoubtedly most important fixture of the 2008/2009 season, the one to which every preceding match has been but a pale prelude – the qualifying match which would not only see England prevail on the scoresheet but also tell us what we, as the English, are and what the Andorrans, those mountainlocked, unshaven wretches who have only recently ceased to scamper around on all fours, are not. It was as satisfying as watching a bulldog swat a gnat with one swipe of its mighty paw, a puff-chested pride of lions bravely bringing down a solitary, tethered ewe, or an enormous steamroller trundling over a grape - a grape that had been spat out and discredited by a member of the English Fruit Standards Authority as unfit for domestic consumption, at that. Small wonder the English fans were in lusty song all evening. Never was there more appropriate occasion to bellow triumphantly than tonight.

The national anthems, as ever, were so indicative of the disparity that the actual playing of the game was extraneous. Our own anthem, rendered with customary monarchistic gusto by our boys, makes one wonder why the good Lord created sexual intercourse when it is so markedly inferior to these verses. The Andorran effort, by contrast, sounded like some sort of requiem to a lost goat, conceived on discarded pieces of lead piping and short lengths of catgut.

The first half consisted principally of England raining chances upon goal as if said chances were homosexuals in a 1970s discotheque song, and it was with a collective "Hallelujah!" that Wayne Rooney's two goals were greeted as he dispatched them, his beaming, bearded countenance as appealing a prospect as hair pie. The Andorrans were, as expected, hampered by playing on a surface larger than the land mass of their own country; it was all too much for their team of part timers, who include among their ranks postmen, shepherds and a fellow who took his leave midway through the second half to reassume his duties as Prime Minister.

Throughout, however, the game was marred by a series of mystifying decisions by the Dutch referee which, as has been darkly hinted at recently in another competition, were almost certainly part of a wider agenda on the part of Europe's footballing bureaucracy, designed to see England depart from the World Cup at the earliest opportunity, lest we ultimately show up the shower of overtanned, hair-stricken, corrupt bunglers who comprise foreigners in general. Still, we persisted in both first and second halves, with intelligent crosses and passes, high to Defoe, low to Crouch. It is a well-known fact that until well into the latter half of the 20th century, most Andorrans believed the football and the moon to be one and the same, plucked from the sky temporarily in order that the match be played. Some of Steven Gerrard's efforts on goal must have rekindled that belief in both their players and travelling fans (who were indeed one and the same).

Finally, England racked up a score so cricketing in nature it would have been perfectly meet for them to have declared in the 82nd minute. Of the Andorrans, this much can be said – their neighbours Spain could take a leaf out of their book. Stand respectfully off England, allow them the space and time to play their game and good football can flourish on the field of play. Harry and pressure them, however, as did the ill-advised Spanish, like European Union gnomes stifling English entrepreneurs with red tape and regulations and churlish, bureaucratic technicalities like numbers of goals counting for more than centuries-old breeding and pedigree, and the creative spark is annulled.

Two things are plain, however – first, that Trades Union rights must be immediately repealed, as they were so successfully in pre-war Germany under Herr Hitler. It would appear that the London Underground strike was conceived out of a not misplaced fear that the spectacle of England's footballing triumph tonight would only bolster the British peoples' resolve that the growing menace of foreign-inspired state socialism be driven back into the sea. They thought they could keep the fans away with their co-ordinated backsliding, but they underestimated the Dunkirk-like spirit of Englanders and their admirable, artery-clogging willingness to travel everywhere by car rather than bow to an authoritarian public transport tyrant.

The second concerns the quite belief-beggaringly asinine decision of the Mr Capello to substitute Wayne Rooney and Steven Gerrard at half time, though it was obvious that they were England's best players. It is in the teeth of such bafflingly arbitrary decisions by this Italian-imported imbecile that England have triumphed in this qualifying stage hitherto, but he has overstepped his bounds once too often. Where is Sammy Lee when you need him the most?

HARTLEY SEBAG-FFIENNES, ARSENAL SUPPORTER

Unlike England, the Republic of Ireland failed to qualify for the 2010 World Cup thanks to an extremely controversial goal involving a conspicuous handball from France's Thierry Henry in the second leg of the play-off. Hartley Sebag-Ffiennes defends the ex-Arsenal player.

WHAT ABOUT THIS HENRY AFFAIR?

L'affaire Henry has dragged on noisily and tediously for some days now, like a Yorkshireman dragging a wooden cart across the cobbles loaded with Hovis, clogs and dripping. Rank and foul has been the air with the dissonant verbal defecation of the halitosis-ridden uncouth, complaining that in the course of passing to team-mate William Gallas there might have been some trifling brush between his palm and the ball. An injustice has been done, they bleat. As one, they cry "'andball", so much so that in some areas of the country, roadsweepers have been pressed into double shifts in order to sweep up the countless dropped aitches. What these buffoons fail to understand, however, is that this debate is about a great deal more than an unimportant manipulation of a sphere. This whole affair is transcendent. It is about culture, honour, architecture. It is not so much about the contact of a man and animal hide but, truly, what separates man and the beasts of the field, or certain of the baser nations for that matter.

One listens, of course, for it is the first duty of the liberal to attend to the disgruntled voice of the common man, even perhaps to nod civilly, concealing if possible the desire to retch. Listen, nod, then dismiss out of hand. (Then shower and massage unguents into the temples in order to efface the unpleasantness of conversing with the unwashed.) We must consider the issue of justice. Yes, there must be justice for all. The Frenchman inside all people of taste tells us this. Justice for all, much as there must be food for all. However, much as there would be little point in presenting a superlatively tossed arugula salad to our aforementioned Yorkshireman, who would doubtless be inclined to take either a watering can or a pair of garden shears to it were you to do so, by the same token there is no point in dispensing the same quality of justice to both the common man and his superior. For the working man, there must be Hovis justice. To the likes of Henry, however, there must be a higher justice – an Arugula Justice, if you will.

It is a shame that Brian Sewell was not the co-commentator on the wireless set, as he might well have offered a more apposite insight into the overlooked aesthetic dimension of this incident. Let us take a leaf from the art critic's book, don our lorgnettes and cast a broader eye upon the stage at large. Yes, technically, by the laws of the game as insisted upon by the punctilious Poujade, M. Henry committed an offence. Yes, in normal circumstances, it is against the rules to handle the ball. But these were no normal circumstances. Had he not done so, not only would the French have stood in danger of missing out on association football's grandest tourney, but the Irish – I repeat, the Irish – would have gone in their stead. Cast the mind back to the idyll that was Camelot and imagine if, due to some footling pedantry, Sir Lancelot had been barred from entering the joust and Squire Seamus elected to take his place in the list field? Armed not with a lance, but a potato and a catapult? Not just the joust but the hastiludes in general would have been reduced to the base, cast carelessly into jeopardy.

It was precisely in order to avoid this contingency that M. Henry was forced to handle the ball. This was Arugula Justice in full and finest effect. It would have been an injustice to the ages for France not to be a part of the 2010 tournament. A World Cup without the French is like a meal without a £500 vintage bottle of Chateauneuf Du Pape – not so much eating as grazing, an impossible prospect for the cultivated to contemplate. Let us, with some horror, contemplate the Irish – shudder at their countenances, forged from the same, rude clay as the Toby jugs from which they imbibe, whose idea of playing the game is akin to hurling a pig's head as far as possible in the direction of a neighbouring village, then hurtling after it in packs, through mud and briar and cesspool, bellowing crude Gaelic imprecations. One does not wish to impugn the citizens of Erin, who in their fictional form exercise a certain poetic fascination upon men of taste and letters. But were their team to have been allowed into the World Cup, Civilisation would have been hurled, not unlike a pig's head, not unlike one of their own long balls, back into the year 1382. The honking, stinking rabble may not understand this – Mr James Joyce, however, that exile and Francophile, most certainly would have. And so, like Zola to the defence of Dreyfus, I cry out on M. Henry's part as he languishes on his own Devil's Island of antipathy, cry out to his persecutors – J'accuse! Let him eat arugula . . .

SELF RIGHTEOUS LIVERPOOL FAN

In January 2010, as an earthquake struck Haiti, calamity too struck Liverpool, who were knocked out of the FA Cup by lowly Reading, plunging the club into crisis.

We've all seen images on our telly screens over the last couple of days that put sport in its proper perspective, reminds us of what true loss and real tragedy is all about. And so, I'd reach and say to fans of Plymouth, fans of QPR, even fans of Man Utd, and say, all right, yeah, so you got knocked out in the third round of the FA Cup but these were just football matches, they don't count for a lot in the wider scheme of things. For serious heartbreak, searing, tear-stained scenes that will stick in the mind and the heart for a long time to come and send shock waves around the world, you only had to turn on the news last night and witness the devastation at Anfield. Liverpool got knocked out in the third round of the FA Cup! It is a tragic loss. The FA Cup without Liverpool is like a wedding disco without "Lily The Pink" by The Scaffold.

This does not happen to this Club. As Jamie Carragher said in that interview with The Echo, "We are Liverpool". There's a serious argument that we should just stop playing games altogether and just Be Liverpool. Specially after last night. I mean, where are we now? Sixth, seventh in the Premier League? In the Europa Cup? Out of the FA Cup? Good enough for Aston Villa, a team with no history, whose fans don't really care whether they win or not on account of not knowing any better and having players that don't play with heart and guts and grit and spittle. Not good enough for Liverpool Football Club. I mean, Reading? I think I speak for most footy fans when I say I'd never even heard of them before last night. I saw the posters up for "Liverpool Reading" and I thought it was gonna be some sort of book thingy, y'know, with maybe Tom O'Connor or Stan Boardman reading extracts from Bill Shankly's biography off of a lectern in the centre circle. The wisdom of that man. The knowledge of that man. "The ball is round, laddie," he once said. "Remember that one thing and you'll not stray far wrong." Or "A football pitch is a simple thing, laddie. A section of grass marked out by white lines. But it's what you do on it, what you do on it, laddie, that's what counts." Or his immortal words of inspiration just before the 1971 FA Cup Final, in that there team talk he gave. "You're a football team, right, aye? Well, then, go out and play football. Oh, and remember – the ball is round." What a God.

See a team like Reading, they don't know nothing about all that. Maybe it's cos they're kids, they've never even hard of Ron Yeats or Gerry Marsden, but the way they played last night, it was, you know, ignorant. It's like they didn't know who they were playing, running around, crossing, scoring, with no respect for the tradition of the Cup and Big Nights at Anfield. No history, no heart, you know, nothing up there, or in there either. As "our" Cilla would say, it's like they didn't know our names and where we come from. And yes, it's as if they'd bundled Cilla Black into the back of a three wheel van to Reading Festival, tarred and feathered her, tossed her around in the moshpit like a rag doll during a set by the reformed Soundgarden then thrown her backstage to be pissed clean by drunken roadies. You do not do that. You piss Cilla clean, you piss me clean.

But hear this – we will rise from the ashes of this setback, as a team, as a city, as a people. We know there is a time for laughter, for Tom O'Connor chuckling about how the vicar always used to confiscate your catapult and gobstoppers on the way into mass – yeah, Tom, we've all been there. This is a time for tears. But tears of resolve. We will stand back, we will bounce tall. We are not afraid to face up to the difficult choices. Here then, is what we will do.

Say "Stevie Gerrarrrrd" a lot, but with redoubled faith and even more "r"s - "Gerrarrrrrrrrrrrrrd".

Deal with Rafa Benitez once and for all. Say to him, look, if this club, this great club, under you, Rafa, drops through the leagues into the Conference over the next few years, make no mistake, there will be murmurings that things have got to improve. Passionate murmurings.

Buy loads of razorblades so as to help out Mr Gillette, one of the club owners, so he might see fit to invest even more money in this great football club which, like the shaving man he is, he liked so much he bought the whole thing, him and that other grand old man from all the way across the sea in the United States, who it is not our place to question.

Finally, though, right now, we need to issue an Emergency Appeal. Whatever you can spare. It's absolutely vital that help gets through to this stricken club. We desperately need to raise funds, so as to sign Pedro Gomez, a promising, 31-year-old centre back who's disaffected at Celta Vigo where he's been playing in the reserves for the past seven seasons. Asking price of £38 million. Another Rafa bargain. Give generously. With heart, with passion, with all your shirt.

ENGLAND V HOLLAND (FRIENDLY)
August 12, 2009

England come from 2-0 down: having uncharacteristically been the recipients of a footballing lesson in Amsterdam, they are redeemed by the introduction of Jermain Defoe, who scores a brace to draw England level. Rare defensive errors from John Terry and Rio Ferdinand. David Beckham sports a rather curious, close-cropped haircut.

EMINENT ENGLAND SOUNDLY TAN HIDES OF HEINOUS HOLLAND 2-2

In a previous report upon this fixture, I offered by way of straightforward factual statement that in contrast with the myriad contributions made by England to Civilisation, including potted jam, Princess Margaret and the Industrial Revolution, the Dutch have given us but one thing – elm disease. Over the next days, it was the task of my manservant Seppings to fetch forth from the letterbox, some two-and-a-half miles down the gravel path from my mansion house, sackload after sackload of letters in protest at this quite innocuous observation. My complainants asserted that, on the contrary, the Dutch legacy in the field of art is prodigious and formidable. I duly journeyed by locomotive to the city of London with a view to inspecting this claim at the National Gallery. And indeed, if I may be permitted to venture into the sarcastic mode, a formidable legacy Dutch art represents. One notes such scintillating works as Cows Graze Near Church, More Cows Graze Near Church, Same Set Of Cows As In First Picture Near Church, Still Grazing, and More Cows Near Church, Surprise Surprise, Grazing. As if these were not varied enough, there was also Bored Woman Sewing By Windowsill and Florid Faced Man Smirks With Self-Satisfied Air Of One Who Has Broken Wind Discreetly And Got Away With It. The latter work was by one Rembrandt, and this was a theme to which he evidently returned throughout his life. One can only hope that the wood in which these daubs were framed was made from already diseased elm, fit for no better purpose. Seppings has been duly thrashed for bringing me such importunate correspondence.

In England, it is the custom of our artists not merely to depict cows grazing but, with manly, New Elizabethan spirit, to cleave them in two - that is precisely what we proposed to do to our foreign opposition tonight. Our national anthem was delivered with such zesty ardour as to warrant a goal awarded in our favour by FIFA's representative in the stands. That he did not speaks volumes about his bias – when up against it, these foreigners stick together. As for the Dutch, with the unpardonable facetiousness of small boys marching up and down in mimicry with broom handles over their shoulders when a military parade passes through town, they pretended to have a national anthem of their own, as if to say "two can play at that game", and had their negro barber-shop quartet make up something on the spot. Next, they will be pretending they have a Queen.

England's line-up was solid, save for the absence of Steven Gerrard, who will be distraught to have picked up a slight injury prior to the game. His commitment to England is undoubted – he would cheerfully break a leg for his country that would put him out for the rest of the season if it gained England but a corner. How devastated he must have been to miss this, what is more than likely to be the most important game of his season. Thankfully, there were stout fellows and true to step into the breach, none stouter than Wayne Rooney – the Dutch defence shrank back from his every attack like small goats in the face of a rampaging elephant on heat. One could almost hear the back four shouting at each other in panic in that language of theirs which reminds of nothing so much as those malformed, aborted foetuses kept in jars in museums of medical science – botched, early efforts at talking properly, long discarded by people of cultivation.

The first half quite clearly belonged to England, whose accuracy in front of goal was unfairly impeded by those ridiculous, Belisha beacon-like shirts Holland insist on wearing, in the glare of whose ghastliness it is impossible to shoot straight. Unaccountably, however, it was the Dutch who scored first. Rio Ferdinand's powers of anticipation and concentration are so high, he had already finished concentrating on this game and was thinking intently about the next one. Hence the backpass which let in Dirk Kuyt, who over the course of the next few minutes, manoeuvred himself into position, advanced a few yards goalward, adjusted his socks, looked around to see that the coast was clear, gauged the target, took aim and shot, past John Terry who had taken over on sentry duty just minutes earlier on the near post. In trying to clear, Terry misfired into his own net, the trajectory of his thigh bringing forth from me a pained ejaculation. Clearly, the goal should not have stood – John Terry wasn't ready – but stand it did. The referee pointed back towards the centre spot, the home crowd erupted, whereupon Ferdinand, alive to the danger, sprang into action and attempted to tackle Kuyt – but just too late. Holland then added a second, which was unwise – for now, our dander was erect.

Fortunately, England's spirits did not wilt. While Signor Capello trilled showtunes from Lady and the Tramp as he prepared a large bowl of pasta Bolognese in the back room, it fell to Stuart Pearce to conjure up the sort of encouraging words that spur stout yeomanry over the walls of our latterday Harfleur. No doubt the players would have taken great heart, as I did, from the flag draped over one of the stands bearing the simple and heartening message "NO SURRENDER". This formulation is as foreign to the Dutch as they are foreign themselves. After all, in order to achieve their capitulation, it is necessary only to arrive at their border in a small detachment of motor cycles and sidecars, wearing uniforms and monocles. Sure enough, Dutch Courage evaporated on England's first serious cavalry charge, with our boys so boisterously abundant with confidence they even let Carlton Cole have a couple of shots, the Dutch tulip bubble now well and truly burst.

Looking back on this victory, one can see the sense, in these security-conscious times, in replacing the real David Beckham for the evening with a fellow evidently procured from an Amsterdam wharf, the sort of heavily tattooed, crudely shaven type whom men of a certain standing in the community but of ambivalent proclivities might discreetly approach, guilders in hand, in order to obtain the sort of satisfaction that cannot be demanded on the steps of one's own club.

The second concerns Signor Fabio Capello, not a "manager" of course, more a lucky charm. However, it is clear from the misfortunes of the first half that his luck has run out. He must be replaced immediately with a fellow of equal or greater amusement value. Might I suggest Mr Bert "Place! Bets! Now!" Kwouk? A capital suggestion, I'd warrant. Failing that, Mr Alan Shearer. Nota bene – the last suggestion was not made in seriousness but represented a second venture into the satirical mode.

ENGLAND V CROATIA (World Cup qualifier)
September 9, 2009

England confirm their passage into the 2010 World Cup in some style, walloping Croatia with an ease that contrasts starkly with their performance two years earlier.

EXCELLENT ENGLAND HAMMER MISERABLE CROATIAN WORMS INTO GROUND LIKE FOUL PIGS 5-1

During the recent Second World War, that key fixture against Germany and the Axis forces, there were those who famously predicted that the whole affair would be over by Christmas. It turned out, however, that they were altogether unfounded in their gloomy pessimism. For although we had Herr Hitler exactly where we wanted him in 1940, so morale-raising and exhilarating an experience was putting the sausage-gobbler to the British sword that we thought it a capital notion to extend the war for five more entertaining years, in order for military historians to have something substantial to sink their teeth into and for Mr Churchill to give full vent to his lugubrious wont in his memoirs.

Such were the feelings of right-minded men as England went 2-0 up in very short order against the swarthy, half-starved whelps of Croatia, who had the look of men who had been hiding out in the mountains for months, surviving by eating each others' faeces. As in 1940, one was heartily glad that there was a good long way to go yet before the final whistle, and plenty of carnage yet to enjoy, what with the systematic humiliating and moral disembowelling of our opponents using the fixed bayonet of our attacking formation. If this had been a boxing contest, it would have been stopped. If this had been a cricketing match, then England would have declared at 2 for 0, before partaking of an early tea. If this had been the Eurovision Song Contest, then Croatia would have been declared the winners by 90 points thanks to points generously awarded them by Bosnia-Herzegovina, Serbia, and Slovenia, but thankfully this is association football and, as such, it is free from all Balkan scheming and men in sequinned knickerbockers caterwauling.

The national anthems had already told their own story, our own bellowed with the sort of stentorian fury that once had Afghani natives scurrying like mice back up the Khyber Pass. The Croatians, by contrast, intoned theirs in a vanquished spirit, eyes darting about as if looking for men in blue berets to whom to surrender rather than take part in tonight's contest. They had no hope of victory, of course; even if they had somehow found a way of prevailing in the goals tally, a gender test on their ear-ringed manager, the like of which has recently brought a certain South African "negress" athlete's performance into question, would surely have seen the decision reversed.

If one could venture a small criticism of the English perfor-mance, in the first half and towards the end of the second, it was that the play was a little intricate. Thankfully, Wayne Rooney, who generally plays in the manner of a lump of sizzling, hairy meat shot from a cannon, redeemed matters with an aimless hoof from his own half shortly before the interval, precisely the sort of blood- and bile-fuelled pointlessness of which the Light Brigade would have approved. We are English Thunderers, not Belgian Lacemakers.

Come the second half and the Croatians, who had, to their meagre credit, at least stood back and formed a guard of honour as England pranced majestically past them in the first half, abandoned all protocol and attempted a few sallies of their own.

However, their best chance fell to Eduardo, a proven foreigner and cheat. Our Glen Johnson was quite within his rights to haul him down manually in the penalty box, lest he attempt another of his infamous dives. This, after all, is a fellow who feigned injury for over a year following a robust and bullish challenge from a Birmingham City player, doubtless with a view to claiming unemployment and sickness benefit, as is the want of Eastern Europeans of his stripe. All this is contrary to the English way, as John Terry, our captain and pillar of inspiration, has pointed out. The English do not dive. Not Rooney, not Gerrard, least of all Michael Owen, equally infrequently Tom Daley.

Thankfully, England went from strength to strength, with more goals from Gerrard and Lampard, inspiring a national cry of: "Why does it always have to be that pair of charmless, glory magnet cocktwats?" I don't think!

A triumph, but allow an old campaigner to issue a warning. We must not be lulled into the complacent assumption that, after this performance, England have already got their hands on the World Cup. We must bear in mind that, first, there is the matter of the ceremony of handing over the trophy. Still, there is plenty of time for this formality to be arranged so as to take place before Christmas.

I further join the chorus of recommendation that this be the last game in which "Signor" Fabio Capello remains in charge of the England team. It is quite astonishing that this absurdly chinned , spaghetti-straining foreign buffoon has actually been allowed a hand in the selection of the team and tactics, as opposed to merely entertaining the team at half time with an accordion. One decision took the biscuit this evening. Emile Heskey was substituted, only for the manager apparently to change his mind and send him back onto the pitch. Seppings later ventured the explanation that in fact he had been replaced by another player, Jermain Defoe. This may be so. However, the confusion he sowed in substituting one player so completely and utterly identical to the other even to the lay eye was immense indeed – it can be no coincidence that Croatia pulled a goal back some minutes later, such was the succour this blunder gave them. With two games to spare, England can now experiment, and the first priority must be to try out a new manager. I would suggest the mysteriously available Mr "Ron" Atkinson, who has shown a much surer grasp of the issues which elude Mr Capello . . .

ENGLAND V UKRAINE (World Cup Qualifier)
October 10, 2009

Already group winners, England rather take their foot off the pedal in this final fixture. There are anonymous performances by one or two "name" players.

EVIDENTIALLY EXCELLENT ENGLAND TROUNCE MUTANT NUCLEAR WASTE PRODUCTS UKRAINE 0-1

Ah, how grand it is to roost at the top of the table, at the top table, so to speak, savouring the exclusive repast of victory, while just beneath you the Croatians and Ukrainians scavenge like refugees on the gravel slopes of inferiority for whatever beetroot or carrot ends you care to strew their way. It was thus for me in 1946 when, as a Major General, I was charged with keeping the querulous Slavic masses in order following the redrawing of that region, as well as taking personal charge of the sex education of their women. As it was then, it is for England today.

It speaks volumes about the backward irreflectiveness of our opponents on the ploughed field of play tonight that they had no idea they existed as a separate people until informed as much by the United Nations in 1990. Since then, they have stumbled along in a sort of oblivious confusion, the gloomy, downturned moustaches of their womenfolk a sign of their base dejection, digging up coal and potatoes for subsistence, eating whichever looks the tastier. Not for them the sustaining English delicacies of battered spam, spotted dick and pickled horse's discharge (a regional dish of my own devising – Seppings, my man, takes five spoonfuls a day at my insistence. It has successfully prevented him from contracting rickets.)

It was with baleful, envious eyes that the Ukrainians looked upon the English team as they lined up for the national anthem. As our boys burst their lungs giving thanks for the continued existence of Her Majesty and, of course, her splendid use of space of a husband Prince Phillip, one sensed that they were the object of a wild, collective surmise from the Ukrainian home crowd, as if marvelling at what splendid forms human evolution might take if you put your best foot forward as a nation. In the case of Wayne Rooney they visibly licked their lips – baked, boiled or mashed, you could see them thinking, he could feed the workers in the garment district of Kiev for an entire week.

Here, after all, was a country who when their floodlights fail due to coal shortages can nonetheless, thanks to the events of 1986, continue to play as they can pick out one another glowing green in the dark. Moreover, the extra limbs I fancy some of their number have sprouted make them a tricky, sneaky proposition for England's honest bipeds. As for their own national anthem, entitled, I shouldn't wonder, More Potato Peelings For The National Grid, Comrades!, it reminded of a Volga boatman breaking wind, slowly, mournfully and pungently, following a dish of borscht.

I should point out that this game was available only by the facility of internet, upon a computing machine. Fortunately, I own such a device – I acquired it in 1947, one of the first in England, and it has faithfully served me since. It fills the entire ballroom in my West Wing, a splendid mass of tubing, valves, knobs, soundboard and ventilators, with a screen one and a half inches by one and a half inches in size. It is operable by bellows, which Seppings worked manually for the full 90 minutes and injury time, pausing only at the interval for a restorative dose of horse's discharge.

The game would have begun at a cracking pelt had not the Ukrainian fans, in all their Slavic wantonness, rained flares on the pitch, one of which almost woke Rio Ferdinand from his early match slumber. Doubtless this was in celebration of this being the 50th anniversary since fire was introduced into this part of the world. It showed admirable restraint on England's part that we did not respond with Stingers and low-flying helicopters dispatching napalm onto the home terraces. Perhaps too admirable. When the smoke had cleared, the Ukrainians claimed a penalty. (I saw no evidence of this – Seppings' left elbow briefly gave out. I had him rub it in thickened horse's discharge, thrashed him, then bade him continue.) The commentator, quite possibly "turned" by his Ukrainian hosts, advanced a quite preposterous tale of a defensive lapse – one of our back four Tommies asleep at the sentry? An outrageous slur, of which UEFA have not heard the last – with our goalkeeper missing, presumably taken hostage by the opposition. England were thus reduced to ten men, with the addition of Steven Gerrard in the line-up making it nine.

Fortunately, the penalty fell to one Shevchenko, who had played in Civilisation for a short time but proved unable to adapt. Memories of his unhappy stay in the land of latrines, non-grey foodstuffs and television programmes entitled "The Nation's 100 Greatest Barns" fazed him in his run-up and he blasted hilariously wide.

The game produced little of note from the Ukrainians thereafter. As for England, Frank Lampard went close twice. Emile Heskey found the back of the net early on. Unfortunately, UEFA churlishly insist that the ball must hit the front of the net, as opposed to bulge the other side having bounced back off the hoardings. Ashley That With Which Yorkshiremen Fill Their Baths* did deflect a ball into the back of his net but I trust that the relevant authorities would not be sufficiently unsportsmanlike curs to insist that such an honest English mistake be made to count against us in the final tally. Carlton Black Substance Dug Up By Northerners Until Mr Scargill Went Too Far* did distinguish himself in his holding up of the ball, while out on the left, Joe Cole was hardly missed.

England, then, complete the "qualifying" rounds, as keen an indignity as Sir Laurence Olivier being required to audition for the part of Othello. And so to Africa, the dark continent, Land Of The Tactically Naïve (well, certainly, it would be tactically naïve of any African team to take to the pitch at all against England) and to South Africa in particular, where, in the tradition of our forefathers, we shall stumble upon natural features of the local landscape which have hitherto evaded the attention of the natives, so downward set are their eyes in desperate, self-absorbed abjection. And so, that table-shaped mountain yonder shall be named Mount Rooney, while the Cape to the South shall, in tribute to our deserving Royals, be duly baptised Cape Princess Michael Of Kent. It is to be regretted that in playing these qualifying fixtures, both our opponents and members of foreign football teams, by the not always happy medium of the television set, will have been given the educative advantage of seeing how the game should be played. Fortunately, being foreigners and therefore disadvantaged, both biologically and phrenologically, it is unlikely that they will take on board any of the lessons we impart any more than they have absorbed correction in the matter of accent and pronunciation. How do we play football? We play the game of football the way we play the game of life: fairly, to the extent that that does not compromise vital British interests; superlatively, though without straying into the womanly realms of embroidery so beloved of some of our intricately-passing, possession-keeping opponents of fluid and questionable gender; and, at all times, victoriously, though as one who recently conducted a motor-car tour of Europe driving on the correct side of the road at all times, I can attest that one is liable to come into harsh and violent conflict with the querulous foreigner when maintaining this incontrovertible fact.

*In the light of the dictatorial edicts of the Politically Correct brigade, I have felt obliged to euphemise and tone down the names of these negroes, lest I be accused of racialist prejudice.

A FINAL ADDRESS FROM THE "WING COMMANDER"

I wish to offer my thanks to zer0 books for willingly agreeing to publish my Match Reports, which I modestly hope will edify the youth of England and the Empire and, I trust, galvanise them to emulate the standards set by their imperial 19th century ancestors. I wish, however, to take this opportunity to disassociate myself strongly from the other titles on this imprint, which I have perused with some horror. These include Mark Fisher's Capitalist Realism: Is There No Alternative? (there is, of course, though it involves the small matter of re-annexing Poland), Nina Power's One Dimensional Woman (this title strikes me as somewhat reductive, denying as it does the duality of the modern female, who is fit both for procreation and the bottling of chutney), as well as Owen Hatherley's Militant Modernism and Dominic Fox's Cold World: The Aesthetics Of Dejection And The Politics Of Militant Dysphoria, which are hardly the sort of volumes I should allow Seppings to read, nor should you your own manservant. It is clear that these publications suggest that revolution, intellectual foment and radical stirrings are in the offing and as such ought to be avoided by all those who hold the interests of Queen and Capital at heart. I should warn both zer0 readers and writers that men like myself are prepared to fight, and fight again for our liberties, which is to say, the liberties we have taken with the lower orders and lesser foreign nations since the days of the Crusades.